STORY AS
A WAY TO GOD

STORY AS
A WAY TO GOD
A Guide for Storytellers

H. Maxwell Butcher

Resource Publications, Inc.
San Jose, California

Editorial director: Kenneth Guentert
Managing editor: Kathi Drolet
Cover design: Ernest Sit
Editorial assistant: Anne McLaughlin

Reprint Department
Resource Publications, Inc.
160 E. Virginia Street #290
San Jose, CA 95112-5848

Library of Congress Cataloging in Publication
Butcher, H. Maxwell (Herbert Maxwell), 1924-
     Story as a way to God : a guide for storytellers / H. Maxwell
Butcher.
          p. cm.
     Includes bibliographical references.
     ISBN 0-89390-201-2 : $11.95
     1. Storytelling~Religious aspects~Christianity. 2. Christian literature
~History and criticism. 3. Christian literature~Authorship. I. Title.
BT83.78.B87 1991
268'.6~dc20
                                      91-2835
                                      CIP

5 4 3 2 1 | 95 94 93 92 91

Contents

PART IV
GOD'S STORY : THE TRINITY

PART V
GOD'S STORY IN OTHER PLACES

PART VI
TELLING GOD'S STORY

PART VII
WRITING GOD'S STORY

Introduction

This is a book for story-writers and storytellers — and for
listeners and readers too. It is for parents and preachers,
educators and entertainers, script-writers and baby-sitters.

It is written because everyone enjoys stories, be they fairy
tales or novels, thrillers or musicals.

It is written because in my experience as a preacher I can
hold my listeners' attention far better with a story than with a
theory.

It is written from a conviction that stories — even fictional
ones — are powerful ways of passing on Truth, and that God is
Truth.

It is not a step-by-step "how-to" book in so many easy
lessons; but I hope that it will help someone to share in the
privilege of telling the story of God.

In some of the following chapters, I may be accused of
being unjustifiably dogmatic. I write as a Christian. If any of my

readers do not share that faith, no doubt they will be charitable enough to pardon my enthusiasm for it.

I have a conviction that there is an Ultimate Truth, which is (in a sense I cannot fathom) personal, and I am content to call that Truth by the traditional word "God." It means, moreover, that I accept the thesis that Jesus of Nazareth (again in a way beyond my understanding) "has made him known" (see John 1:18). Jesus called God his "Father," and authorized his followers to do the same (Matthew 6:9). More than that: in experience as well as in theory, I believe that the ghastly death of Jesus led to an unprecedented resurrection, and I have learnt by experience that he changes human lives for the better. He himself described this work as the work of "the Holy Spirit" (John 20:22).

It seems to me that the terms "Father," "Son," and "Spirit" are metaphors for truths that our human minds cannot comprehend. The modern tendency to avoid the masculine in referring to God is perhaps a sensitive reaction to sexist language; but it is also a presumption that we know more than Jesus did. So if my use of these terms offends any reader's sensibilities, I can only ask for forgiveness.

The same applies to my use of the library of ancient books that we call "the Bible." It is without doubt the work of human writers; but I accept it also as "God-breathed" (2 Tim 3:16), and therefore, authoritative in matters of faith. This extends to its historical accuracy, especially that of the four gospels. If the writers' cultural milieu distorts their historical accuracy, I do not believe that this was intentional. Their aim, no doubt, was to preach rather than to produce biographies; but that very preaching was rooted in history. We have no "life of Christ" more accurate than the one in the Bible.

Even if the Bible were in fact fictitious, it is still a story that has gripped the imagination and loyalty of millions of readers. It has produced through many generations a faith in that Truth that we call God. My purpose in writing this book is simply to help the storytellers of this generation to express in their own words the timeless story of God.

H. Maxwell Butcher

PART I

WHY TELL A STORY?

Chapter 1

The Power of a Story

"It won't work! We'll never get the message across!"

"I know. This book will never sell. After all the hours we've spent on it . . . "

It was at the height of the Cold War. The speakers were two much-traveled Americans with a burden for their country.

"If we could only make people see what we've seen!"

"Well, if we can't, the Soviets are going to trample right over us. Here we are, pouring millions of dollars into Third World countries . . . "

"Yes, but in such a ham-handed way! *They* don't make the mistakes that we do."

"So the Communist steam-roller will keep straight on, right across Asia, simply for want of some good P.R."

"That's what this book is meant to be — public relations — telling our own people what the United States is doing to better the world . . . "

" . . .and all the wrong ways we're doing it. Remember when . . . "

"That's it!"

"What's it?"

"'Remember when!' That's it! Instead of a bundle of reports and statistics, why don't we write a story — a story of all the bumbling officials we've met, and the ridiculous gaffes they've made?"

"Why? Because we'd be sued for libel, that's why."

"No — I mean write it as a novel. *Invent* a country. Write things exactly as they happened, but mix them up, so that everybody can recognize himself, but nobody can pin it on us."

"And another very good reason why not. We've already got a manuscript ready for the press, and it's due in six days."

"So scrap it! Start over! We'll have to work as we've never worked in our lives, but we can do it. We won't preach — we won't exhort — we'll simply tell a story, and let the story do its own work."

That conversation is fictitious, but the facts are not. William J. Lederer and Eugene Burdick did scrap their manuscript. They did write a novel in six days. It was published as *The Ugly American.*[1] It was summarized in *Reader's Digest* within a year. It caught the imagination of readers across America and beyond. Best of all (if the reports are true), it was this book that moved President Kennedy to launch the Peace Corps as a means to counter the failings described by Lederer and Burdick.

As a novel, the book is very loosely woven. It is little more than a series of short stories, mainly about the fictional country of Sarkhan. Here are some incidents:

> An enthusiastic young American set up a powdered milk depot to raise the living standards of the Sarkhanese. Unexpectedly he meets an old comrade who saved his life from the Japanese during the Second World War. Now the two friends are on

opposite sides. The man bears no personal animosity, but he is a Communist, committed to advancing the revolution *at all*. That involves discrediting the United States.

His method is to force his friend, at gunpoint, to mix poison with the milk, and so spread sickness among the women and children. When the American refuses, the women are told that he had already done so. Their revenge — thousands of tiny scratches, and a "Rapist" note pinned to his bare chest — land him in hospital. There the American ambassador dutifully visits him and warns him to keep his slate clean in future. The Ambassador makes no attempt to discover the truth.

In another story Homer Atkins, an American engineer whose acknowledged ugliness helps to keep him humble, invents a water-pump. It is powered by pedaling a bicycle and saves Sarkhanese farmers the endless labor of hand irrigation. At once he enters into a partnership with Jeepo, a Sarkhanese who supplied one or two ideas, and who recruits salesmen. Everyone concerned profits, but no one is a profiteer.

Homer's wife has a different sort of success. Noticing that Sarkhanese women's backs are bent from years of house-sweeping with the short-handled reeds of the area, she constructs a broom from the longer reeds she has discovered. Instead of telling the ladies that her method is better than theirs, she casually lets them see her using the new labor-saving broom. In a short time long-handled brooms appear everywhere.

Another incident tells about a shipment of supplies being unloaded in a Sarkhanese port, a gift from the people of the United States of America. While the American ambassador ceremonially accepts the gift, a Sarkhanese sentence is stamped on every sack: "A gift from the people of the Soviet Union." Nobody at the American embassy, of course, can read Sarkhanese.

Why did these stories, with their grim humor, have such a powerful effect on us? Clearly the authors were right: a story carries far more weight than a statistic; but why? What is there about a story that "works"? According to Marcus Barth,

> The telling of a story, if well done, makes the listeners wonder, gaze, laugh, shake — but it *leaves free* both that which is narrated and the audience . . . Stories can move to action.[2]

They do not attempt to "master" either the subject or the listener. Still more forceful are Robert McAfee Brown's words:

> A story must reach me on some level to which I can respond, but it must "stretch" me, pull me beyond where I am now, open up some new door of my mind or heart.[3]
> Stories can change us, turn us about, be instruments in a process that can be called "conversion."[4]

It was conversion that *The Ugly American* was aiming at.

[1] Eugene Burdick and William J. Lederer, *The Ugly American* (New York: W.W. Norton & Company, 1958).

[2] Marcus Barth, "The Cowboy in the Sunday School" *Religious Education* Part I (January/February 1962), 43; Part II (March/April 1962), 126.

[3] Robert McAfee Brown, "My Story and 'The Story'" *Theology Today* Vol XXXII No. 2 (July 1975), 167.

[4] Ibid., 172.

Chapter 2

The Political Message

If a story, even a fictional story, can have such a powerful impact, think of what a good storyteller who has a political axe to grind could achieve.

The technique is as old as the hills. Early in the Old Testament there is the story of Jotham whose whole family had been murdered by the usurper Abimelech. Jotham shouted from a hilltop his fable about the trees who "went out to choose a king" and elected the bramble: the result was disaster for them. Abimelech, the king, evidently understood the reference to himself.[1]

In our own century, two novelists have quietly defied the authorities, one in South Africa, the other in Soviet Russia, by the simple power of their novels.

Alan Paton's *Cry, the Beloved Country*[2] is set in the South Africa of apartheid. Nowhere does Paton say, in his own words, "apartheid is wrong;" the narrative is enough.

A black African pastor watches helplessly the destruction of his son Absalom, who has become a *tsotsi* – the local name for a lawless inhabitant of gangland. The pressures of his adolescent need for freedom, the repressive race laws, and the challenge of the militant leaders have caught him in a vise. When at last he murders a white man, the best efforts of a white lawyer are not sufficient to save him from hanging. The old father is more aware of his weakness than of his strength, but he knows something of the power of prayer. The story ends with the father keeping a night-long vigil of prayer before the execution. He knows that in spite of what happened, there is still a future.

Inevitably the reader's sympathy is with the father. Even the boy, murderer as he is, is not the villain of the piece: that title belongs to the social system that has spawned *tsotsis*. Neither Absalom nor his father ever existed; Alan Paton invented them; and yet thousands have been crushed by these same forces. The old man doomed to despair, and the young man doomed to death, are fictitious only in detail. The plot could have happened. It does happen.

Of course, there was no need to clothe the idea in fiction. It would have been just as effective (though perhaps more dangerous) to tell literally the stories of Africans caught in this whirlpool of destruction.

Trevor Huddlestone did just that. The effectiveness of his book *Naught for Your Comfort*[3] lies not in political theories, nor in invective against the government, but in documented examples of repression and persecution. He told stories of what he saw and the world listened, to the intense displeasure of his government.

A similar battle cry is heard in another work of fiction: *Doctor Zhivago*[4] by Boris Pasternak. The target this time is the oppressive force of the Soviet Union.

> Yuri Zhivago is a successful doctor, sympathetic to the aims of the Russian Revolution, but caught in its aftermath and tossed on the scrap heap of humanity. The nation moves on, but Zhivago, together with a million others in real life, loses his purpose and his identity in the process. His wealthy upbringing tells against him; ironically, the one man who stands by him, an anonymous figure in the shadows, is his politically acceptable half-brother.
>
> His marriage breaks down when his wife prefers exile in France to life under the new regime. A common law alliance with a woman whom he knew in the old days is followed by another with someone who is as lost in the dregs of society as he. His career, which could have been so brilliant, and which included selfless service in the Soviet army, finishes in the gutter. The Revolution, in its liberation of the ordinary person, has destroyed someone of extraordinary goodness and strength.

Who will ever be able to say which were more powerful, the stories of fact or the stories of fiction? Probably both kinds of stories played their part in dismantling apartheid and in the growth of *perestroika*, for both took the rest of the world by storm, and so stood as a challenge to the governments concerned.

[1] Judges 9:8.

[2] Alan Paton, *Cry, the Beloved Country* (New York, Charles Scribner's Sons, 1948).

[3] Trevor Huddlestone, *Naught For Your Comfort* (London: Fontana Books, 1957).

[4] Boris Pasternak, *Doctor Zhivago* trans. Max Hayward and Manya Harari (London, Wm. Collins Sons and Co. Ltd., 1958).

Chapter 3

The Spiritual Message

If a story can have a political message, it can just as well have a spiritual one, for example, *The Sound of Music*.[1] It starts with a true episode in the life of a real person.

Maria (does anyone remember that she had a surname before she married Baron Von Trapp?) is a young woman whose life in a convent is as sincere as it is stormy. Before her final vows she is appointed governess to the seven children of a naval officer whom she later marries. The Nazi coup sends the family fleeing from their home in Salzburg, together with a young curate, whose skill in training a choir led them to a new life and musical career in America.

Her own memoirs are told in *The Story of the Trapp Family Singers*[2] and *A Family on Wheels*.[3] The account that captured the imagination of the public was the musical comedy on stage and the film, *The Sound of Music*.

Something changed between the happening and the telling. Baroness von Trapp told, as factually as she could, the incidents of her employment, marriage, escape, and subsequent life. Rogers and Hammerstein did otherwise. They took the outline, with its dramatic sequence, and made it into a work of fiction.

The Baroness herself was consulted during the creation of the stage production and she was invited to the premiere showing. In spite of some misgivings, she was pleased with the final result.

When the musical was produced as a film, it was different. She wrote to the producer with some criticism of details in the play. His telephoned answer was: "We are not concerned about persons and facts. I haven't read your book, and I don't intend to. We are more or less going to make up our own version of your story."[4] Maria was furious, but the matter was out of her hands.

The sequel was amazing. The film was so unlike reality that any spiritual message she had tried to include could well have leaked through the cracks. In her memoirs she had written: "There I stood — my God and I — on a new threshold of life."[5] God was real to her, powerful, guiding, strengthening. The film had changed God into a lovable but utterly unreal person, just as the convent was lovable but utterly unreal. And yet, surprisingly, God was not unreal to the viewers. What might have been just a melodrama turned out to be a film of power. Baroness von Trapp writes about

> ...the uncountable number of letters from all countries of the world, telling me that looking at the film *The Sound of Music* has strengthened their trust in God, or has made them think for the first time in their lives that God is somebody who could be trusted.[6]

What happened? God the Savior refused to be left out of the film version for God was the principal actor in the original events. God survived all the changes in the script: the night-time escape from the Trapp mansion, the hoodwinking of the Gestapo, the hide-and-seek in the convent, and the tinkering by a nun with the engine of the pursuers' car. All this fiction is no more than a screen on which the truth is projected. Maria wrote that she wanted to fold her hands and say from the bottom of her heart, "'Dear Lord, thank You for *The Sound of Music.*'"[7]

[1] Richard Rogers and Oscar Hammerstein, *The Sound of Music,* 20th Century Fox, 1965.

[2] Maria A. Trapp, *The Story of the Trapp Family Singers* (New York: J.B. Lippincott Co., 1949).

[3] Maria Augusta Trapp with Ruth T. Murdock, *A Family on Wheels: Further Adventures of the Trapp Family Singers* (Philadelphia: J.B. Lippincott Company, 1959).

[4] Maria von Trapp, *Maria* (Carol Stream, Illinois: Creation House, Inc., 1972; paperback, New York, Avon Books, 1973), 214.

[5] Ibid., 72.

[6] Ibid., 218.

[7] Ibid.

Chapter 4

Guess What

Why should a story have any message at all? Or, if a writer has something to teach, why make it obvious?

Dorothy L. Sayers had very definite views on this subject. She was already well-known as a writer of detective novels when the British Broadcasting Corporation commissioned her to write for their program, *The Children's Hour*, a series of twelve plays on the life of Jesus. When these plays were published under the title *The Man Born to be King*, she wrote in the long preface:

> The dramatist must begin by ridding himself of all edificatory and theological intentions. He must set out, not to instruct, but to show forth; not to point a moral but to tell a story.[1]

He must, she adds,

> ...trust the theology to emerge undistorted from the dramatic presentation of the story.[2]

Whether Sayers obeyed her own rule is doubtful. She seems to have had "edificatory and theological intentions." She not

14

only was providing drama for*The Children's Hour*, she was preaching. The difference between Lord Peter Wimsey, her detective hero, and the Lord Jesus Christ, the central figure of her play cycle, is not in her literary skill but in her theological purpose. Her intentions are clear, and her theology does "emerge undistorted" from the plot, without any need on the author's part to point the moral.

But here is a novel whose intentions are far from clear. There is certainly a message to be heard, a lesson to be learned, but it is by no means certain which of many possible lessons the reader will find (nor which lesson the author had in mind). The novel is William Golding's *Lord of the Flies*.[3]

A party of boys, traveling by plane in wartime, have crashed on an island. No attempt is made to explain why their compartment contained no adults. In fact, the plane crash is only a device to make logical the existence of a group of boys on a deserted island.

At first you meet two, Ralph, whose sense of responsibility makes him see himself as a natural leader, and "Piggy," a fat, short-sighted boy urgently needing the security of approval. Drawn into friendship by their circumstances, these dissimilar boys begin to organize a society out of the many others whom they encounter on the island. Ralph's great ambition is to build a fire big enough to be seen by a passing ship, and so to engineer a rescue.

Before the rescue, however, a different group gains the ascendancy. Traveling together as a choir, these boys have already formed a cohesion among themselves and a loyalty to the senior choirboy. Their main thought is to hunt down wild pigs for food.

The rivalry between the choir group and Ralph's supporters turns into bitter enmity. The fighting is on

a schoolboy level, until Piggy, blind from the loss of
his spectacles, is hit by a boulder and hurled off the
rocks to his destruction. His is not the only life lost.
A loner named Simon, whose inability to communicate is more than matched by his courage, explores
the summit of the mountain. Simon searches for the
mysterious "being" known to frequent the mountain.
The boys' fear has led them to sacrifice pigs' heads to
the creature. All that Simon finds is a dead airman
caught in the bushes by his parachute. But as Simon
stumbles back to tell the others of this truth, he is mis-
taken for the "evil thing" himself. The mob of boys
who club him to death dare not admit even to themselves that they recognized him.

What does all this mean — if there is a meaning deeper than
the fiction? Is Golding telling us how religion started? Are all
our sacrifices as pointless as the pigs' heads, and every deity a
"Lord of the Flies"? Is Simon a picture of Jesus Christ? Or is
this whole tale a plea to return to political sanity? Suppose we
ask the question: "What would happen if we could start again,
with the innocence of childhood, without the prejudices that
have silted up the channel of history?" — would this book be a
reasonable answer? Have we learned from it that human nature
is irredeemably depraved? Or that there are mysteries outside
this desert island that we call the universe, and our sojourn here
will one day be cut short by intervention from outside?

Golding answers nothing of these questions. He has said
what he wanted to say, and the reader has heard — not
necessarily what he hoped the reader would hear; and has
responded — not necessarily in ways he could have foreseen.
The story stands as its own justification.

When you lay down the book, the reader has been "stretched," "changed," perhaps even "converted." Such is the power of a story.

[1] Dorothy L. Sayers, *The Man Born to be King: A Play-Cycle on the Life of our Lord and Savior JESUS CHRIST* (London: Victor Gollancz Ltd., 1943).

2 Ibid.,19-20.

[3] William Golding, *Lord of the Flies* (London: Faber & Faber, Ltd., 1954).

PART II

WHAT MAKES A STORY?

Chapter 5

The Pattern

The ingredients of a story are, of course, events — events of fact or of fiction, events in the memory or in the imagination. A story has to be *about* something, and about something that happens.

It is no use collecting events and setting them down higgledy-piggledy. They need to have a pattern. In fact, a story might be defined as the pattern that we see in events.

Jean-Paul Sartre has an incident in his novel *Nausea* that seems to have no pattern at all.

> The husband, amused and mysterious: "Say, did you see that?"
> The woman gives a start and looks, coming out of a dream. He eats and drinks, then starts again, with the same malicious air: "Ha, Ha!"
> A moment of silence, the woman has fallen back into her dream.
> Suddenly she shudders and asks: "What did you say?"
> "Suzanne, yesterday."

"Ah, yes," the woman says, "she went to see Victor."

"What did I tell you?"

The woman pushes her plate aside impatiently. "It's no good."[1]

Of course the man and the woman know the pattern; we do not. The whole point of it, as Sartre tells it, is that it is meaningless.

Now read and compare these sentences from the Bible.

> When Methuselah had lived 187 years, he became the father of Lamech. And after he became the father of Lamech, Methuselah lived 782 years, and had other sons and daughters. Altogether, Methuselah lived 969 years, and then he died.[2]

Perhaps you find this boring; but it is not meaningless. The events are carefully selected to show a pattern. It is assumed, for instance, that the family descent is carried on through the first born son. The author omits Lamech's brothers and sisters for the very good reason that they add nothing to the story. Or again:

> Abraham was the father of Isaac,
> Isaac the father of Jacob,
> Jacob the father of Judah and his brothers . . .[3]

And later, much later in the list, another Jacob was

> . . . the father of Joseph, the husband of Mary, of whom was born Jesus, who is called Christ. Thus there were fourteen generations in all from Abraham to

David, fourteen from David to the exile to Babylon, and fourteen from the exile to the Christ.[4]

Matthew visualizes history as a divinely ordained pattern, whose focus is Christ. The preparation for his birth falls — no doubt by God's intention — into three periods of fourteen generations. Another writer might take these same facts and read into them a different meaning. The same genealogy would then yield a different story.

Not always — not usually — is the pattern of a story so simple or so obvious. If it were, we should soon stop listening. Or should we? Perhaps the story of our ancestors is as important as any that we could find. James A. Michener, in his novel *Hawaii*, speaks of these same "Begat" passages as the favorite Bible reading of the Hawaiians.

> There is much in the Bible that we do not understand [he makes Kelolo say]. How could we? We don't know the many things the white man knows. But when we hear The Begats it is like music to our ears . . . because it sounds just like our own family histories, and for once we can feel as if we, too, were part of the Bible.[5]

" . . . as if we, too, were part of the Bible": that is what makes the narrative live.

Ian Ramsay, the late Bishop of Durham, England, and a former college chaplain, wrote:

> The primary task of education must be to teach insight . . . when and as we discern a work which has "come alive" in some particular situation.[6]

Just as the "Begat" passages came alive for the Hawaiians, because the pattern was familiar to them, so every storyteller has to find the pattern that resonates with the listeners' or readers' imagination. The next chapters describe something of how this pattern is discovered.

[1] Jean-Paul Sartre, *Nausea* trans. by Lloyd Alexander, Introduction by Hayden Carruth (New York: New Directions Publishing Corporation, 1969), 48.

[2] Genesis 5:25-27

[3] Matthew 1:2

[4] Matthew 1:16-17

[5] James A. Michener, Hawaii (New York: Random House, 1959), 29.

[6] Ian T. Ramsey, "Christian Education in the Light of Contemporary Empiricism," *Religious Education* (March/April 1962), 95.

Chapter 6

The Culture

Biblical critics have a way of attributing the authorship of certain books to "schools" of writers. They seem to forget that even in a school of thought the writing must be done by persons. Did you ever hear of a best-seller written by a committee? Even if the group agrees on what needs to be said, someone has to take the initiative and put the words down on paper.

Yet there is truth in this idea of communal authorship. Lowther Clarke, in his one-volume Bible commentary, says of the sources of the Pentateuch:

> The Hebrew method has been the normal way of writing a book in other nations at a certain stage of development . . . . There was no word for "author" in Hebrew, which was content with *sopher*, scribe. The message was all-important, the person who delivered it immaterial.[1]

The Pentateuch came into being, like other sagas of antiquity, as one or more gifted persons expressed the fears, the thoughts, the aspirations of a whole nation, of a whole culture. First by word of mouth, then in writing, and now with all the accessories of printing, of computers, of television, the memories of communities are preserved.

Doctor Zhivago was written by Boris Pasternak. It was also written by the Russian people. It emerged from the struggles of a nation in a time of creativity and agony. Pasternak is, it is true, not a spokesman for the Soviet state. He rebelled against, rather than expressed the thought of his nation. He stands in relation to the Soviet Union much as the Hebrew prophets stood to their people: a hurt lover. He and they name the deep longings of their people, no less because they find a name that is unpopular. The story-teller may be "the voice of the people" without the people ever recognizing the voice.

The culture shapes the story: the story also shapes the culture. Take, for instance, the *Ramayana*. No one knows much about its author, Valmiki, but his book lives as one of India's great epics. It is called "his book"; in fact, he never wrote it. He wrote the original core, to which accretions have clung like barnacles.

Aubrey Mennen, whose whimsical reconstruction of the plot for English speaking readers may or may not recapture Valmiki's meaning, writes:

> Unfortunately, generations of Brahmins have rewritten
> his poem so that in parts it says the opposite of what
> Valmiki plainly intended.[2]

According to Mennen, Valmiki was a "skeptical realist" who rebelled in thought against Brahmin ascendancy. The

Brahmins in turn captured his story and made it theirs. Like
Pasternak, this writer was a spokesman of his culture, or
perhaps a prophet against it.

For many centuries the culture has been molded by the
book. Two of the most common names among the Hindus are
Ram and Sita, after the hero and heroine of the book. Illiterate
villagers know of the Prince who went into exile in the woods,
of the abduction of Sita by Ravana, and her return to her
husband. They know it because of the annual *dasehra* festival,
with its ten days of rejoicing in their heroes' memory. They
know it because of the *katha* – a word often translated as
"song," but with the specialized meaning of "a story told in
song by a professional bard." And so the story, like the village
fig tree, continues to put out new leaves. The story and the
culture continue to influence each other.

Two thoughts occur. If the story can so change and be
changed by the culture that is its matrix, how much do we
Christians alter the great story of Christmas by our celebrations
– yet how little would Christmas mold the culture if we did not
keep the holiday? How long would it take *Doctor Zhivago*, under
appropriate pressure from the government, to evolve into a
Communist apology?

It is, of course, possible for a writer to describe the culture
from the outside. This would involve steeping oneself in the
culture until one thinks the thoughts of that nation and that
century. James Michener is a master of this. His novel *The
Source*[3] takes us through Israel's history from humanity's first
consciousness to the present day. It is impossible to say for
certain: "The author's religion is this, or that." Sometimes he
clearly disapproves of a matter, as in his story of the Crusades,
where his sympathies are with the ineffectual Count Volkmar,

not with the Count's riotous, ungodly brother-in-law, nor even
with the pious and short-sighted priest whose diaries keep
record of the disaster.

But there is so much that he approves of! When Michener
writes about old Zadok the Patriarch, he describes his
conversations with El Shaddai as if he himself believes in El
Shaddai. To judge from the chapter, "The Saintly Men of
Safed," Michener must be a loyal Jew, staunchly defending the
Torah. But his picture of Mark (born Menahem) makes the
reader feel that only in conversion to Jesus Christ lies true
freedom. Michener immerses himself in his subject, and so
brings the varied and successive cultures of the land and its
inhabitants to life for us. He is not a part of the culture, but he
enters it in thought. The culture is still the matrix of the story.

But "culture," or even "community" is too vague an entity
to hold center stage in the telling of a story. The culture is
merely the backdrop against which the players are seen acting
out their parts. And in the next chapters we shall move on from
the backdrop to the players themselves.

[1] The Rev. W.K. Lowther Clarke, *Concise Bible Commentary* (New York: The
MacMillan Company, 1953), 335.

[2] *The Ramayana as told by Aubrey Mennen* (New York: Charles Scribner's
Sons, 1954), 4-5.

[3] James A. Michener, *The Source* (New York: Random House Inc., 1965).

Chapter 7

The Hero and the Storyteller

Harvey Cox begins his book *The Seduction of the Spirit* by saying:

> All human beings have an innate need to tell and hear stories and to have a story to live by.[1]

He illustrates this by telling something of his own story, but he does not define his meaning, "A story to live by." Surely we all have stories, communal stories and personal ones. How can we *need* to have a story to live by? Cox is saying two things: first, that we need to have a firm root in the society that bred us, a sense of identity within our culture, of continuity with our past; and second, that from that root we need to branch out into our own story. Out of the many possibilities we develop our own environment, and live our own life. Conforming to or rebelling against the *given* of our communal story, we interpret the events that mold us, and in turn mold our surroundings and ourselves.

We twentieth century Westerners are an individualistic bunch. We care little for our tribal identity: we "do our own thing," and for many of us that robs life of meaning. It is as if in our urge to be ourselves we opt out of our community. In *The Homeless Mind* Peter Berger and his colleagues speak of the "modern trends that have left the individual 'alienated' and beset with the threats of meaninglessness."[2] They say in different words the same thing as Cox, that unless the episodes of our life have a continuity and a purpose we are sick. To be more precise, unless we can identify, as least subconsciously, their continuity and purpose, we are sick. We must be able to write our own story.

Sartre's novel *Nausea*, (see chapter 5) is the story of a man without a story. Sartre, as novelist, traces the pattern — a jumbled pattern, an aimless pattern, but a pattern none the less. The story is sufficiently clear for Sartre to carry the reader's interest with him. The hero Roquentin can find no pattern at all. He feels his life to be as disjointed as the overheard conversation.

> Roquentin is researching for a historical book, without any clear idea of why he must write it. Indeed, nothing seems important to him. He wanders about the dim-lit town, encountering familiar people, but never meeting them on a personal level. Whatever happens, he is only a spectator. Every now and again he has an overwhelming feeling of nausea, which at last he analyzes as no more and no less than a horror of "existence." The roots of trees exist, in a particular shape, with no reason except that they are there. The child-murderer whom he happens to see, and later read about in the paper, is just as much someone who exists, with no relevance whatever to

him. He clutches at his friendship with the "Self-Taught Man," however boring, and at his old love affair, now burnt out, with Anny. Nothing means anything any more. Things and people simply exist, and it makes him feel sick. Like "the tramway that passes in front of the Hotel Printania in the evening," life "does not catch the reflection of the neon signboards; it flames up for an instant, then goes on with black windows."

How can a man with so little meaning in life be the hero of a novel? Through the skill of the author. Sartre finds a pattern where his hero has none. The storyteller is the one who traces the pattern running through other people's lives, and expresses it in through a choice of words, who interprets to the listeners or the readers the reality that has been there all along, unseen. The storyteller is the visionary who can bring into focus the blurred image, the artist who can set down not only what is apparent, but what can be perceived behind the visible.

A key ingredient in a story, then, is a hero (or a villain) with a life-pattern that is at least clear to the storyteller. A commercial literary agent gives this advice to writers in a "Commercial Plot Skeleton:"

> Underlying nearly all commercial fiction is the commercial plot skeleton: a sympathetic protagonist finds himself in trouble, and tries to extricate himself, but all his efforts instead just get him deeper into difficulty, with each obstacle more menacing than the last — until, when things seems worst, he uses his own efforts and character to get out of trouble.

> This is not a *formula*. Instead, it contains the basic
> ingredients for nearly all successful fiction of all types.
>
> When this skeleton is inverted, the lead character is a
> villain who succeeds in evil doings until, at the end, he
> fails.[3]

It may be questioned whether this is the only pattern for
fiction. Sartre makes Roquentin neither hero nor villain. What
the skeleton makes clear is the need for a central character, and
a storyteller who can make sense out of the character's life.

To do that requires deep sensitivity. It requires the ability to
stand inside the spirit of the protagonist. Frank S. Stuart did
this brilliantly in *City of Bees*,[4] using as his hero not a human
person but a swarm of bees.

> The constitution of the colony, its organization
> and day-to-day operations, and the seasonal cycle of
> its life, are described as if the insects were human ac-
> tors with human emotions. The ecstasy of the queen
> bee's mating, the fury of the battle with an invading
> swarm, the ruthless execution of a mouse that wan-
> dered in, make this story as fascinating as it is
> beautifully told. You are aware, even as you enjoy it,
> that this is a fantasy. You cannot really penetrate the
> secret springs of a bee's feelings and motives: Stuart
> has made us believe that it can be done.

It is like this, too, with a human person's story. You cannot
glimpse more of inwardness than that person allows you.
Through the understanding of your own story you can make
analogies with another's. Provided that you have a secure base

on which to stand, you can cast outward that magic noose, imagination, and capture the events that make up the other person's pattern. The wider your experience of life, the more clearly you will perceive the story mutely told to you and the more realistically you will repeat it back to that person or to your listeners and readers.

[1] Harvey Cox, *The Seduction of the Spirit: The Use and Misuse of People's Religion* (New York: Simon and Schuster, 1973), 9.

[2] Peter Berger, Brigitte Berger and Hansfried Kellner, *The Homeless Mind: Modernization and Consciousness* (New York: Random House, Inc., 1973, Paperback: Vintage Books, 1974), 196.

[3] *Commercial Plot Skeleton*, Broome Agency Incorporated, Box 3649, Sarasota, Florida 33578.

[4] Frank S. Stuart, *City of the Bees* (London, George Allen & Unwin, Ltd., 1947).

Chapter 8

The Story of a Story

Here is the story of a story.

One of the popular Walt Disney cartoons is *The Jungle Book*,[1] with its cast of a jungle-dwelling boy and his lovable friends the animals. It is well-known that this is film is taken from the book of the same name by Rudyard Kipling. Nor is it a secret that the training of the junior boys in the Boy Scout movement — the "Wolf Cubs" or "Cub Scouts" — was adapted from that same book. The film was a box-office hit, but it was a body-blow to the Scout movement, for Disney made comic what Kipling made great.

It is less well-known that Kipling in turn drew on previous accounts. A little known history of an orphanage started in India by a missionary society in the last century contains the telling quotation:

> In the "Register of Admittance into the Secundra Orphanage" there is on Page 2 the following entry:
>
> No. 96   Date of Arrival   State of Health

Dina Sanichar	February 4th, 1867	Idiot.
By whom sent	Form where sent	Baptized
Magistrate	Agra.	Sept. 27, 1877

| Cause of removal | Date of removal |
| Death. | October 18th, 1895 |

| Remarks | Died of consumption. |
| Wolf Boy. | Buried by Rev. W. McLean[2] |

Of the wolf-boys of Sikandra — for there were several —
Dina Sanichar was the only one to reach maturity. These boys
were very different from Mowgli of the Seeonee Wolf Pack.
Without exception they appeared to be mentally retarded, and
no wonder. That is, they were mentally retarded from the point
of view of the historian of Sikandra, who wrote as an English
educator. They may well have been, like Mowgli, mentally
advanced from the wolves' point of view. Kipling entered,
through imagination, the thoughts and feelings of the animals
and of Mowgli himself. He took the reports of real children
who were smoked out of wolves' dens and found in them a
different pattern from that in the Sikandra register. And so the
story developed.

A number of boys and girls were discovered in various parts
of India being reared by wolves. They were "rescued" and
introduced into human society, to which they found it hard,
often impossible, to adjust. The national press reported these
incidents and they passed into history.

Rudyard Kipling the Tale-spinner transferred the fact into
fiction. He also interpreted the fact in a very different fashion to
suit his purpose, which was presumably, to entertain.

Rudyard Kipling the Britisher was a spokesman for the culture that overran half the world, and India with it, yet rarely does he let his imperial patriotism intrude into his story. The spirit that sent British administrators to ruin their health on behalf of the "uncivilized" of the world, the spirit of team-work and of fair play, breathes through every chapter. It is expressed best in "The Law of the Jungle," in such verses as this:

> As the creeper that girdles the tree-trunk the Law runneth forward and back —
> For the strength of the Pack is the Wolf, and the strength of the Wolf is the Pack. [3]

Lord Baden-Powell, searching for a motif for the junior boys in his Boy Scout movement, found in *The Jungle Book* the ideal mixture of play and learning, of adventure and truth. Walt Disney Studios rediscovered the magic of the story, and like Kipling, adapted it to entertain, in their own inimitable style. Now it is part of a new culture, the pretend-culture of the feature cartoon.

The story is now so far removed from its origin that our natural reaction is to say: "But of course it isn't true. Boys don't really grow up with wolves."

1 *The Jungle Book*, The Walt Disney Co., 1967.

[2] F.J. McBride and F. W. Hinton, *Sikandra* 1840-1940 (Agra: The Sikandra Press, 1940), 198.

[3] Rudyard Kipling, *The Jungle Book* with illustrations by Aldren Watson, foreword by Nelson Doubleday, 2 Vols. (New York: Doubleday & Company, Inc., 1948), Vol. I, 91.

PART III

WINDOWS ON GOD

Chapter 9

Comedy

According to Sallie McFague TeSelle, "In a sense any story is about ourselves."[1] If she means that all narrative is autobiography, then of course she is wrong. If she means (as of course she does) that all narrative reveals something of the author's sense of values, then she is right. To put it differently — perhaps to show the other side of the same coin — every story is about God, as the storyteller sees God.

For a moment forget all that you have learned about God, and start afresh. People have such widely differing ideas about Him (some people might say "about It," or even "about Her"). I think that the only thing that they all have in common is that God is the Ultimate. Anything less is not God: it is "a god." If you will accept this as a working definition of God — that whatever is Ultimate is God — then look at several different styles of writing, and see what each has to say about who or what God is. These styles are called by their correct, if difficult to pronounce name, "genres."

The first genre is *comedy*. Comedy is a recognition, a
celebration, of the absurd. Against the background of an
ordered world some incident, some personality, stands out as
different. It tickles our awareness, and we laugh.

Comedy tells us a great deal about God. The God of the
comedy-writer is a very good God. To begin with, in a comedy,
the very absurdity of the plot or of the characters implies that
life is not absurd. God is a God of order, and it is those things
that break the established order that are funny — and then only
if they are relatively harmless.

Comedy is healing. Laugh till the clouds lose their grayness
and the sun comes out! Enjoy the absurdity of a farce, and even
worries become a little less overwhelming. "Comedy is an
escape," wrote Christopher Fry, "not from truth but from
despair; a narrow escape into faith."[2]

Or again, the comedy-teller can be a pricker of bubbles, a
demolisher of idols; comedy may be not so much an aberration
from reality as a reminder of reality in a world that has become
pompously unreal. Jesus' parable of the laborers in the
vineyard[3] is not only a challenge to social justice and an allegory
of God's grace. It is also in invitation to laugh — to laugh at the
discomfiture of the earlier laborers, to laugh with the
unfortunates who have the tables turned in their favor, but most
of all, to laugh because there is a mercy that laughs at too strict
a justice. *There* is God: the Merciful as well as the Righteous.

We do Jesus a disservice if we fail to watch for the twinkle
in his eye as he speaks of camels' and needles' eyes, [4] or fish
with coins in their mouths.[5] The author of *Godspell* [6] thought
so, and set the audience laughing not at, but with Jesus. And
(for the Christian at least) a sense of humor in Jesus implies a

sense of humor in God — a sense of humor in the very composition of the universe, in the heart of Reality.

But Jesus' laughter is a foil to his seriousness, not a substitute. Comedy is not enough to portray God. It may indeed be part of God's make-up, but it cannot be the whole. A God who cannot laugh is terrifying: a God who does nothing else is a fool.

Comedy also may be a way of running away from God, rather than a way to seek God. "I fled Him," wrote Francis Thompson, "under running laughter."[7] Saki's short stories are sometimes uproariously funny, but often they have a vein of gruesomeness peeping through that leaves a sour taste behind. Take for example his tale of "Esmé" the hyena that followed two fox-hunting ladies. The hyena was tame enough to enjoy the ladies' company, but also enjoyed as an evening snack a gypsy child who was picking blackberries. ("I don't suppose in many large encampments they really know to a child or two how many they've got," was the Baroness's conscience-soother.[8])

We laugh with Saki, who makes it sound so ridiculous, so impossible; but what if it really happened? Saki is saying that the horror of life is too grim to look at, save through the smoked glass of comedy. Saki's comedy reveals nothing of the goodness of God. God is indifferent, or else a tyrant.

Comedy cannot bear the weight of an ultimate. When an ultimate is hung on it anyway, it ceases to be comedy. If there is no order against which to view life's oddities, then the whole of life is an oddity. *Alice in Wonderland*[9] would be a horror story if it came true.

You remember the story of the little English girl who follows a white rabbit down its hole, and at the bottom finds a strange new world, where animals speak, where you eat and drink things that make you grow or shrink at an alarming rate. A caterpillar puffs at a hookah; nursery rhyme characters come alive; a Cheshire cat fades away until only its grin is left; a sheep stands behind a store counter, knitting; and at last Alice finds herself on trial by the King and Queen of Hearts.

Of course, the whole adventure turns out to be a dream, which at once makes it credible; for what strange inversions of reality take place in our dreams! The whole point is that such a topsy-turvy world is *not* reality. At least, we assume it is not; but how do we know? Some people find reality just as unreal. Sartre sums it up through Roquentin's lips:

> Nothing that exists can be comic . . . The word absurd-
> ity is coming to life under my pen . . . All that I could
> grasp . . . returns to this fundamental absurdity.[10]

Nausea is only one of many novels that have assumed the ultimate absurdity of life. Kafka's *The Castle*[11] reads like a comedy, but some scholars include it among the modern tragedies. It can be classified as an example of that modern phenomenon, the "Literature of the Absurd."

In *The Castle* a man is summoned to act as Land Surveyor for the Castle. The Castle is situated high and inaccessible above the village. The whole story consists of his attempts to contact the people at the Castle and his discovery, through his relations with the villagers, of the enormous complexity of the Castle's bureaucracy. The Castle is completely separated from village life. They are two worlds, interrelated, perhaps, but for ever apart.

The sheer frustration of the Land Surveyor's position belongs to the world of comedy, because life is not really like that: laugh and enjoy it. But no. On the contrary, Kafka is telling us even as he smiles that life is very much like that. Read the novel thoughtfully and you will find an allegory. God is as inaccessible as the Castle. Reality is as remote. Absurdity is the beginning and ending of our existence. In the planned ending of this unfinished novel, the hero (known only as "K," who is Kafka himself) was to die with his quest still unrealized. Absurdity taken to the ultimate degree leads to despair.

Comedy then, reveals in its author a conception of the "Truth" — of "God" — that may be true, but not complete; or if comedy is the narrator's complete view, then it is hopeless. But there are other genres which need to be explored.

[1] Sallie McFague TeSelle, "The Experience of Coming to Belief," *Theology Today* Vol. XXXII #2 (July 1975), 159.

[2] Christopher Fry, as quoted by Robert G. Boling, *Enquiry*, (March/May 1975).

[3] Matthew 20:1-16.

[4] Matthew 19:24.

[5] Matthew 17:24-27.

[6] Stephen Schwartz, *Godspell*, 1971.

[7] Francis Thompson, "The Hound of Heaven," *The Oxford Book of Modern Verse 1892-1935*, ed.W.B. Yeats, (Oxford: The Clarendon Press, 1936), 54.

[8] H.H. Munro (pen name "Saki"), "Esmé." in *The Second Century of Humor* (London: Hutchinson & Co. Publishers Ltd., [undated]), 699 ff.

[9] Charles Ludwidge Dodgson (pen name Lewis Carroll) *Alice's Adventures in Wonderland*, (London: 1865)

[10] Jean Paul Sartre, *Nausea* trans. by Lloyd Alexander, Introduction by Hayden Carruth (New York: New Directions Publishing Corp.,1969). See chapter 5 footnote 1.

[11] Franz Kafka, *The Castle*, definitive ed. trans. Muir, Willa, et. al. (New York: Schocken Books Inc. 1974).

Chapter 10

Melodrama

Fairy stories traditionally begin: "Once upon a time" (which really means "this never actually happened"). They end "and they all lived happily ever after." Most adult stories have the same ending, not in words, but in the denouement. Everything comes out right in the end.

It may be oversimplifying to classify all happy-ending stories as "melodrama." It is safer to assert, however, that, like fairy stories, they happen "once upon a time." No one can guarantee that life will turn out "happily ever after," but the reader feels let down if the hero dies miserably in the last chapter, and so the author brings everything to a happy conclusion. Remember that "Commercial Plot Skeleton" quoted in chapter 7? "When things seem worst, it is the hero's own efforts and character that are used to escape trouble." Or if the hero fails, it is because the hero is actually the villain, so we are glad for the failure.

Take the *Western* as an example. Marcus Barth describes the Western as a morality play.[1] It has, he reminds us, "good guys and bad guys". The good guys are heroes. Goodness demands action, and is always rewarded — i.e., there is Law in the world. Excellent! This means that God is Righteousness, Justice, Law. Unfortunately, in our adult experience, good has been known to fail, to be shattered, to be mildewed by cynicism.

The same description could apply with more or less truth to romances, pulp novels, gothics, many films and most television serials. They come from the never-never land of "happily ever after." Or it can be called the "sometimes-sometimes" land. The happy ending is not of its nature untrue. Love stories can develop happily, and many a life survives the storm clouds to enjoy the evening sunshine. The fallacy lies in the *certainty* that this must be so. In melodrama, disappointments are allowed, but they must be temporary. Reality is Security and Hope.

Now a Christian may well reply that the above is a very good description of God. Hope is one of the abiding realities in I Corinthians 13:13. In Romans 8:28 "We know that in all things God works for the good of those who love Him." Yes, but Christian experience suggests that there is much more to God than that. A line in the *Rubáiyát of Omar Khayyám* sums up well the God of the melodrama: "He's a good fellow, and 'twill all be well."[2] Such a description diminishes God, denies experience, aborts reality. For this reason "happy ending stories" tend to be escapist. Like comedy, they teach us a great deal of truth. They lead us nearer to a God who is really God, but they are not enough.

There are echoes of melodrama in the Bible. A psalmist stated bluntly: "I was young and now am old, yet I have never seen the righteous forsaken or their children begging bread."[3]

The tale of Job, despite Job's outright defiance of God, has what Lowther Clarke calls "the conventional happy ending."[4] It was Jesus who, both by his teaching and by his deliberate choice of death, shocked his followers out of their easy assumption that suffering is always a punishment, and that good people will come out all right in the end.

One memorable line of *Jesus Christ Superstar* parodies the whole philosophy of melodrama. It is when Jesus is on his way to trial. The crowds, yesterday adulating him and now following his arrest with the unconcerned interest of television viewers, tell him, "You'll escape in the final reel." [5]

How remote from the fact! True, there is in the film version a hint of resurrection. While the other actors return to their bus without Jesus, a shepherd is seen leading his flock across the sunset (or is it a sunrise?) Who is he? Why is he there? Has Jesus come back to life? Viewers, answer that yourselves: we are not going to tell you. Similarly *Godspell* closes with the same joyful, playful, life-giving "Prepare ye the way of the Lord" with which it opens — but who sings it? Has Jesus returned? Is there another prophet to take his place? Has the gang he brought into being realized that even his death cannot quench life? No answer. Find out for yourself.

There is a happy ending in both these dramas, but it is not the conventional one. Both *Godspell* and *Superstar* have rejected melodrama as the clue to Jesus' story. Even if either of them were able to follow him through to his resurrection, resurrection is not "escaping in the final reel."

Jurgen Moltmann has strong words to say about this. He starts his book *The Crucified God*, " . . . from the assumption that Jesus died with the signs and expressions of a profound abandonment by God. Easter does not solve the riddle of the Cross, but makes Christ's Cross a mystery."[6]

This is in line with Moltmann's own experience.

> Shattered and broken, the survivors of my generation were then (1945/49) returning from camps and hospitals to the lecture room. A theology which did not speak of God in the sight of one who was abandoned and crucified would have nothing to say to us then."[7]

Jesus, by his death, makes sense of our own desolations; but he makes nonsense of the certainty of "living happily ever after." There must be a place, our experience tells us, for the hero who perishes. There was for Jesus, and there will probably be for us, no "escaping in the final reel."

[1] Marcus Barth. "The Cowboy in the Sunday School." (Part II) *Religious Education*. March/April 1962, p. 120.

[2] Edward Fitzgerald. "Rubáiyát of Omar Khayyám of Naishapur." stanza 64

[3] Psalm 37:25.

[4] T. W.K. Lowther Clarke. *Concise Bible Commentary*. New York: The Macmillan Company, 1953 , p. 64.

[5] T. Tim Rice (lyrics), and Andrew Lloyd Webber (music) *Jesus Christ Superstar* (Leeds Music Limited, 1970); from the sequence "The Arrest".

[6] T. Jurgen Moltmann. *Der Gecreuzigte Gott* (Munich: Christian Kaiser Verlag. 2nd ed., 1973) translated into English as *The Crucified God. The Cross of Christ as the Foundation and Criticism of Christian Theology* by R.A. Wilson and John Bowden (London, S.C.M. Press Ltd., 1974), 181.

[7] Ibid., 1.

Chapter 11

Tragedy

So we come to *tragedy*.

An irresistible force meets an immovable object: what then? That is the problem facing an author with the courage and the integrity to follow the characters to their conclusions, as Pierre Boulle has done in *The Bridge over the River Kwai*.[1]

> The immovable object is Colonel Nicholson, "brilliant officer, disciplinarian, perfectionist, whose passion for duty led him to perform an almost impossible feat of military genius for the Japanese Army he hated"[2] — namely, the building of a bridge that was to be the final connecting link for the Singapore to Burma Railway. The irresistible force is "Force 316," a dedicated group of British soldiers trained in sabotage. Their immediate objective is the destruction of that same bridge when the first train crosses it. The ending, if not predictable in detail, is inevitable: death to the heroes of both operations.

Tragedy, in the literary sense, is not simply disaster; it is the clash of inflexible forces leading to disaster. The Greeks defined tragedy as "the war of the gods"; we, insignificant mortals, are caught in tensions beyond our handling. Shakespeare put the same thought into the mouth of Glo'ster in *King Lear*:

> "As flies to wanton boys are we to the gods;
> They kill us for their sport."[3]

Thomas Hardy quoted these lines in his preface to *Tess of the D'Urbervilles*, a novel in which he deliberately defies what he calls "avowed conventions."[4] Tess Darbyfield is raped or seduced by a distant cousin, Alec D'Urberville. It is not clear whether the author distinguishes between the two; certainly to her fiancé they amount to the same thing. She is rejected on her wedding night. She lives a life of degradation and poverty, and she eventually murders Alec. She is hanged, the inevitable punishment for a killer. Hardy, in a much quoted and misquoted sentence, says, "'Justice' was done, and the President of the Immortals, in Aeschylean phrase, had ended his sport with Tess."[5]

Clearly the cause of the this tragedy is human sin — Alec's, not Tess's. Underneath this story, however, is a view of the Universe in which God (if God exists) treats created beings as playthings.

The same thought runs through Albert Camus' *The Plague*.[6]

The city of Oran is quarantined because of a massive outbreak of bubonic plague. A handful of people caught in this death-trap, are described. Their heroism and their cowardice, their loves and their jealousies are projected on a giant screen of final disas-

ter. The hero, Dr. Rieux, knows that he can battle the
disease, and perhaps survive it. He *does* survive, but
the plague always lies dormant, undefeated, ready like
a beast to pounce again on defenseless human beings.

It takes intellectual courage to write a book like this. Camus
is like his own character Rieux, standing heroically in the face of
inevitable death. He cannot identify with Fr. Paneloux, the
priest who interprets the plague as "the will of God"; but
neither does he ridicule him. For, if such a destruction can
occur, what might God be like? Did God cause it? Or is God
powerless to prevent it?

Sinclair Lewis wrote a similar and dissimilar tale of plague.
In *Arrowsmith*[7] the tragedy is caused not by an impersonal fate,
but as in *Tess*, though less obviously, by human sin, by the
character of the participants.

Young Dr. Arrowsmith is confident that he has
found an antidote to plague and pleased to have a
chance to test it in a real epidemic. Unfortunately, if
his test is to show scientific results, it requires retain-
ing a "control group" of untreated people, a group
condemned to a painful death. To the doctor, the important thing is that one day the world will be free of
plague; to the sufferers, it is imperative that they receive the antidote at once. Arrowsmith's motive (and
the cause of medical science) is in direct opposition to
the good of the people among whom he is working
(and the cause of compassion). Which one points
more accurately to God? Is God also caught in the di-
lemma?

Tragedy, like comedy, recognizes the absurd, but instead of laughing it off as a superficial exception to an ordered universe, tragedy sees absurdity at the core of everything. Whether it exists as sin in the human will, as disaster in the forces of nature, or as evil in the demonic realm, the absurd cannot be avoided. It always leads to suffering in one form or another. Further, it poses a great problem: perhaps the Ultimate is evil. Perhaps God is a devil. How can we deny that our experience of the world is full of the stuff of tragedy?

If you take tragedy to its final limit, you have hell, the condition of utter hopelessness. There is a tantalizing glimpse of hell in Sartre's play *No Exit*.[8]

> Three people are locked together in a room. There is no punishment, no torture — and no exit. Only slowly does it dawn on the audience that all three have died, and that this is their afterlife. There are many touches of humor, but it is none the less a tragedy because of its hopelessness. There is no angry God or gloating devil; only a trio eternally tormented by their unfulfilled desires for one another. *No Exit* is an extension of the frustrations of life into eternity.

C.S. Lewis treats the same theme differently in *The Great Divorce*.[9] Hell here is no less tragic, but the book is not a tragedy because there is hope.

> An excursion bus is setting out from hell to heaven (late, of course; nothing works very well in hell). Anyone is free to make the tour and of those cu-

rious passengers who go, none is compelled to return. Almost all choose to do so. Everything in
heaven is too real for their taste. The grass pricks
their feet, the apples prove to be golden, and too
heavy to lift, the light hurts their eyes. They prefer to
return to the isolation and unreality that they chose
in their earthly life.

Whether or not Lewis is right in suggesting that there may
be another chance after death, he cannot escape from this
tension: that hope is as much a part of our experience as
despair. Tragedy does not give us a complete picture of God: for
it shows God as a Tyrant, and some of us have experienced
God rather as a Lover. There must be something beyond
tragedy.

[1] Pierre Boulle, *The Bridge over the River Kwai* (New York: Bantam Books,
1957).

[2] Ibid., back cover.

[3] William Shakespeare, *King Lear, Act IV, Scene 1*.

[4] Thomas Hardy, *Tess of the D'Urbervilles: A Pure Woman*, originally published
1891, republished with introduction by Carl J. Weber (New York: The
Modern Library [Random House Inc.] 1951), xxix.

[5] Ibid., p. 508.

[6] Albert Camus, *The Plague*, (New York: Alfred A. Knopf, 1969).

[7] Sinclair Lewis, *Arrowsmith* (New York: Harcourt Brace and World, Inc.,
1925).

[8] Jean-Paul Sartre, *No Exit and Other Plays* (New York: Vintage Books Edition,
1955).

[9] C.S. Lewis, *The Great Divorce* (New York: Macmillan Publishing Co., Inc.,
1946).

Chapter 12

Beyond Tragedy

> Short of damnation, there can be no Christian tragedy.
> If a person writes a tragedy of the classic type, Christi-
> anity must be kept out of it. . . .Where Christ is,
> cheerfulness will keep breaking in.[1]

So wrote Dorothy L. Sayers in the introduction to her radio
plays, *The Man Born to be King.*

For the Christian, Reality is Resurrection. God is the one
who cares and rescues, using even death itself as a method, and
transforming death into life. God is, as Moltmann insists,
involved in Jesus' death, as in every tragedy. There is no escape
from tragedy: there is escape *through* tragedy. The resurrection is
not an avoidance of the cross: it is its natural outcome.

Therefore, for Christian writers at least, and perhaps for
others, there is a class of literature that faces tragedy in all its
gruesomeness, but does not stop there: it moves on beyond
tragedy. There is no name for this genre; perhaps "Resurrection
Literature" would be the clearest term.

M. Kristin Rayment, in a useful paper on Tolkien, draws
attention to Tolkien's use of the "good ending, which is
characteristic of a certain genre of novel."[2] She quotes Tolkien:

> The sudden joyous turn is not essentially "escapist" nor
> "fugitive" . . . it does not deny the existence of . . .
> sorrow and failure; the possibility of these is necessary
> to the joy of deliverance; it denies (in the face of much
> evidence, if you will) universal final defeat and in so far
> is *Evangelium*.[3]

It is not easy to write Resurrection Literature. It requires
great integrity to prevent its falling back into melodrama. It
takes courage also, since a writer has to face the tragedy of the
characters. Christian novelists walk a tightrope between tragedy
and melodrama; whether they keep their balance is a matter for
disagreement.

Eugenia Price, for example, fails in *Lighthouse*. She eases her
agnostic hero into a position on the newly formed church
vestry, and persuades him to take his beloved wife's faith more
seriously.

> One evening not long after they became a part of the
> fellowship of Christ Church, Janie insisted that he hear
> the children's prayers for a change.
> "You don't know what you're missing, dear, by not
> hearing your own children ask God to bless their papa
> and keep him safe from harm."
> "All right, ma'am." He laid aside his newspaper. "But
> you wait for me right there in the chair. I suspect a trick
> anyway," he teased. "Think you might get your old
> husband to say a word of prayer, too?"[4]

The situation is human enough, but it is an extra laid on
the surface of a romance that is excellent without it. It does not
reach the status of Resurrection Literature. James Gould
achieved his ambition; he also found marital happiness and
service to others. His slow and partial Christian conversion is
not an integral part of the plot. Like him, we suspect a trick
anyway. We suspect it even when we read in the "Afterword"
that both characters and plot are historical.

On the other hand, we suspect nothing in Elizabeth
Goudge's *Green Dolphin Street.*[5] Here we know we are reading
fiction, even though the mainspring of the plot was suggested
by a factual incident. We expect to be reading a romance; we
know that everything has to come out right in the end. It comes
as a shock, therefore, to find that God has had a hand in this
story. God achieves a happy ending through the very thing that
nearly ruins the hero's life.

> William Ozanne's atrocious memory for names
> leads him to propose, by mail, to the wrong girl.
> When she arrives, after a journey half round the
> world, he has the honesty to marry her. Their family
> life is disastrous, and his real sweetheart — his wife's
> sister — becomes a nun. She learns to pray for un-
> known people by picturing in her imagination scenes
> that are actually taking place, without her knowledge,
> in her sister's family. It gives the reader a start to real-
> ize that her prayers are answered even as she makes
> them. God is one of the characters in the fiction, and
> God behaves as one expects, never coercing people
> against their will, but steering them to ultimate recon-
> ciliation. Indeed, in William's dogged determination

to keep faith with his wife, there is a strong hint of Jesus' "obedience unto death."[6]

Not all Christian stories are Resurrection Literature, and not only Christians can write Resurrection Literature. After all, if God is the kind of Savior that Christians believe in, God is not limited to rescuing those who believe in Jesus. It is very possible to experience the grace of God without knowing from where it comes.

One Flew Over the Cuckoo's Nest,[7] is a very different novel which, in my opinion, achieves this status. Here is no Christian propaganda. It is a lurid account of a raw slice of life.

Into a mental hospital ward comes a new patient, the swaggering, swearing, whoring Randle Patrick McMurphy, transferred from jail. In a very short time he has conned his way into the leadership of the "acutes," the "chronics" and the "vegetables" that make up the ward population. He also has become the implacable foe of the establishment, in the person of the senior ward nurse. To Nurse Ratched, he is a disturbing influence, destroying her well-planned therapeutic program. He, in turn, sees her as a manipulative martinet.

His great contribution to the ward is to treat his fellow patients not as cases, but as persons. Under his laughing, bantering encouragement each grows in self-confidence and spiritual stature. Each takes a tentative step toward wholeness. His methods, typically unorthodox, include a fishing trip with a prostitute as chaperon, followed by a night's orgy with two girls smuggled into the ward.

Inevitably the tension mounts toward tragedy. Yet
when death comes, it has been cheated of its victory.
Two patients who commit suicide do so because they
cannot face a return to their hopelessness after catch-
ing a glimpse of something bigger. Nurse Ratched
seems to have won the feud when, her voice destroyed by his strangling hands, she orders his
lobotomy. McMurphy returns to the ward vacant, broken. Miss Ratched comes back to write out her orders
at her desk. It is then that "Chief" Bromden, the big
Indian who used to be the butt of the ward, does the
sanest act of his life. He smothers what is left of
McMurphy with a pillow and makes his escape. The
closing words of the book are symbolic: "I've been
free for a long time."

A less likely "Christ-figure" it would be hard to imagine. No
one is called to admire McMurphy's morality or his tactics, nor
yet his murder at Bromden's hands. It may be misleading to use
the word "resurrection" in connection with this novel, which
leads not to life, but to death. And yet, when death has passed
by, death is no longer a tragedy. McMurphy's own death, like
that of Jesus, has been both the logical outcome of his actions,
and the means of freedom for his brothers.

[1] Dorothy Sayers, *The Man Born to be King*, 27.

[2] M. Kristin Rayment, "Editorial," *Pacific Theological Review: Resources for Ministry Today* (Spring 1977), 2.

[3] M. Kristin Rayment, "Inklings of the Good Catastrophe," *Pacific Theological Review: Resources for Ministry Today* (Spring 1970) 20, quoting from J.R.R. Tolkien, "On Fairy Stories," *Essays Presented to Charles Williams*, 81.

[4] Eugenia Price, *Lighthouse* (Philadelphia: J.B. Lippincott Company, 1971, (Paperback, 1972), 333.

[5] Elizabeth Goudge, *Green Dolphin Street* (Toronto: Hodder & Stoughton Limited, 1944).

[6] Philippians 2:8.

[7] Ken Kesey, *One Flew over the Cuckoo's Nest* (New York: Viking Press, Inc., 1962).

PART IV

GOD'S STORY :
THE TRINITY

Chapter 13

God of Action: the Father

Does God have a story?

It is hard to imagine a story without episodes, and hard to think of episodes except in terms of time. Events happen one after another. But, so we are taught, God is eternal. Are there episodes in eternity? We do not know.

Jews and Christians do know that God chose, according to Exodus 3:14, the name "I am." That in itself allows for many interpretations. Paul Tillich spoke of God as "absolute being" — in other words, *we* exist, and have our little stories: God *is* — indeed, the very fact of "being" is God.

That may be so. If it is, God cannot have any sequence of events. Events *exist* against the backdrop of unchanging *being* of God. That view is challenged by many experts when they interpret the Hebrew word for "I am." Lowther Clarke writes:

> 'I will be what I will be' is a more probable translation.
> Yahweh was always to the Hebrews the God of action;
> that action will be self-determined and self-consistent.

'I am,' suggesting pure essence, sounds too metaphysical to be right.[1]

Perhaps there is truth in both views: God eternally *is* and God continually *acts*. But there is often an intolerable tension between the two. For example, it is easy to fall into the trap (which Tillich carefully avoids) of thinking of God as simply a part of nature. God *is* – in the universe; God *is* – in the crops; God *is* – in the reproduction of plants and animals and human beings.

Kosuke Koyama's fascinating book, *Waterbuffalo Theology*,[2] sheds much light on this. Koyama, a Christian living in a land of Buddhists, describes Buddhism as cyclical, in rhythm with the seasons, in harmony with death and rebirth, in tune with the song of nature. This is *not* the same as saying that God acts. It is the opposite. It is saying that nothing ever really *happens*. Year in, year out, God rolls with the punches and slumbers.

This idea is challenged both in the Old Testament and the New. The old religion of Baal, which was waiting for the Israelites when they arrived in the Promised Land, is a long way from modern Buddhism, but many of its assumptions are the same. The Israelites were fresh from an overwhelming experience of God in Action – a God outside the universe, beyond nature, but who takes the trouble to act within the human sphere of time and space. The Israelites saw in the devastation of Egypt coincidences that defied any other explanation except that God had acted. They had watched the thunder cloud descend on Mount Sinai and had been welded into one nation, a chosen nation, by the action of God. In the Promised Land they were confronted by a religion in which God could be manipulated by the appropriate sacrifices, where human beings could act as they pleased, because God never acted at all. God just existed. The sphere of Baalism is nature; the sphere of Israelite religion is history. No wonder prophets like Elijah would have no compromise. "If the Lord is God, follow him; but if Baal is God, follow him."[3]

A similar tension exists in the New Testament. The Hebrew view of God acting is opposed by the Greek view of a God whom we can understand by our own philosophies. Gregory Dix put it this way:

> For all forms of Syriac thinking [i.e., the 'Eastern' way of thinking, which includes the Israelite religion] the ultimate explanation of life lies *beyond* history and time altogether — in God, conceived of as 'the living God.' In Hellenism [i.e., Greek thought] this was not so. Its 'humanism' seeks to understand life solely from within life, from the rational observation of men and things and events . . . it is always apt to explain God from nature and human life, not nature and human life from its conception of God.[4]

God, then, according to Hebrew thought, stands outside creation, and acts on it at will. Events are the result of God's choice. To quote Gregory Dix once more,

> [The Book of] Acts, like the Gospels, is written throughout with a strong sense of the *sacredness* of the concrete facts it narrates, because the author believes that it is through what actually happened that the 'counsel of God' was manifested and fulfilled.[5]

We in the Western world are heirs to the Greek way of thought. The humanism that Dix spoke of is everywhere today. Ludger Schenke wrote,

> When we today hear that a miracle has happened, we think: The laws of nature have been broken. In those days [Dix would have said 'in that way of thinking'] one thought differently: The Deity has acted![6]

So God as revealed in the Bible is primarily the God of Action, the God of history. God writes a story across the world and across the centuries. That does not answer the question, "Does God *have* a story?"

God has. What story God has in eternity we cannot say; in time, the story of God turns on the fulcrum of Jesus' incarnation, Jesus' death, Jesus' resurrection. Perhaps that is partly what John meant when he said: "The Word was made flesh and dwelt among us, and we beheld His glory"[7] — yes, and we also beheld God's story.

[1] Lowther Clarke, *Concise Bible Commentary* (see chapter 1, fn. 5), 359.

[2] Kosuke Koyama, *Waterbuffalo Theology* (Maryknoll,New York: SCM Press Ltd.), 1974.

[3] I Kings 18:21

[4] Gregory Dix, *Jew and Greek: A Study in the Primitive Church* (Glasgow: Dacre Press, 1953), 10.

[5] Ibid., 39.

[6] Ludger Schenke, *Glory and the Way of the Cross: The Gospel of Mark*, trans, by Robin Scroggs (Chicago: Franciscan Press 1972), 40.

[7] John 1:14.

Chapter 14

Jesus of Nazareth: the Son

There has been a spate of books written in the last few generations searching and researching the story of Jesus. There are attempts at finding the "historical Jesus" behind the alleged fictions of the Gospels. There are "Lives of Christ," novels and films of the life of Christ, harmonies of the Gospels: for whatever we surmise about the Eternal Father, the Son has a story that is very much part of our human, historical scene.

Jesus knew his own identity, and wrote his own story. The point at which he first knew himself to be the Son of God remains for us one of the mysteries of the hidden years. Who knows whether Mary told the facts of his conception to the growing boy, or whether his awareness grew out of his intimate prayer life? By the age of twelve he was already planning to write his Father's story into his own.[1] The great chapter that opened in his thirtieth year would have been tragedy, if the tempter had been able to persuade him to revise the plot. It seems clear that Jesus planned his own career, and even his death, by referring to the Old Testament. His radical reinterpretation of some of its themes does not negate — rather it reveals — the authority that he saw in it. His deliberate surrender to death shows his implicit faith both in its prophecies of resurrection, and in its commands to obedience. If we see Jesus' story as the visible focus of God's story, Jesus evidently saw his life a part of a broad narrative, which encompassed all Israelite history.[2] His New Covenant was a descendant of the Old, not a breaking away. His Church was a reconstruction of the congregation of Yahweh. His promise to return "with the clouds of heaven"[3] is taken by most Christians to mean that the final chapter of his story is yet in the future.

In him, then, all the ingredients of a story described earlier fit together perfectly. He is the hero and the storyteller; he interprets his own culture — the long history of Israel —and from it builds a new culture — the centuries-long, world-wide Christian church. He chose, not his heredity, of course (or did he?) and only in a limited way his environment, but he chose what he would make of it. His is the story above all stories.

It is difficult to arrange in order the many episodes that make up the story of Jesus, but the broad outline is clear. Its beginning is remembered every Christmas; its ending every Easter — its earthly beginning and ending, that is. Its eternal quality is as mysterious as that of the Creator.

It appears that he grew up almost entirely in the obscurity of Nazareth, although attempts have been made to show that He visited England or India. Only after he reached thirty did he hear from the wings of the cosmic stage his cue: "John is baptizing." Jesus took over what John was forced by his arrest to lay down, but he widened the range of his message. No longer was the call: "The Kingdom of Heaven is about to come!" but "The Kingdom of Heaven has arrived!"[4] For a few hectic months he attracted huge crowds in the Galilee, his home province. His fame made it necessary to trek northward for a holiday, and it was at Caesarea Philippi that for the first time one of his followers claimed outright that he was the "Coming One," the Messiah. From then on he deliberately shocked the public by his word and actions, shaking off the crowd of admirers until only a few stalwarts stood by him, as he strode purposefully to Jerusalem and the death he knew awaited him there.

The best known part of his entire story, except perhaps his birth, is his arrest, his death and his return to life. His death and resurrection are perhaps what he himself saw as the purpose of his existence. It is this that Paul and others took up later as the focal point of the religion that grew out of his story.

Paul has a wonderful summary of the whole tale, starting from eternity, ending in eternity, touching time like a great parabola intersecting a straight line.

> Though he possessed the nature of God, he did not grasp at equality with God, but laid it aside to take on the nature of a slave and become like other men. When he had assumed human form, he still further humbled himself and carried his obedience so far as to die, and to die upon the cross. That is why God has so greatly exalted him, and given him the name above all others, so that in the name of Jesus everyone should kneel, in heaven and on earth and in the underworld, and everyone should acknowledge Jesus Christ as Lord, and thus glorify God the Father.[5]

Here is Resurrection Literature at its truest and grandest, form. Here is the great fact that makes Resurrection Literature true. God is the One who saves through tragedy: God has demonstrated the fact in the resurrection of the Son. The story of God is the story of Resurrection.

[1] Luke 2: 41-52.

[2] John 5:39, Luke 24: 44-45.

[3] Mark 14:62.

[4] Matthew 3:2, Luke 4: 17-21.

[5] Philippians 2:6-11; *The Complete Bible, An American Translation*, Old Test. trans. J. M. Powis Smith, et al, New Testament trans. Edgar J. Goodspeed, (Chicago: The University of Chicago Press, 1923).

Chapter 15

God in Action: the Spirit

The whole Bible is the story of God, and for Christians the story of Jesus of Nazareth is its climax; but it does not finish there. God is bigger than the Bible. God writes a story across the pages of history through others besides Hebrew prophets and Gospel writers. Early in the Christian era Justin Martyr wrote:

> I declare that I prayed and strove with all my might to be found a Christian, not because the teachings of Plato are contrary to those of Christ, but because they are not in all respects like them; as is the case with the doctrine of the others, Stoics, poets and prose-authors. For each discoursed rightly, seeing that which was kin to Christianity through a share in the seminal divine reason (Word).[1]

God is at work in all people at all times; and "God-at-work" is a good description of the Holy Spirit. We can cooperate with or resist God, but God continues to write the story. Therefore it should be possible to discern that story at any point in human experience.

Of the many books written about the Holy Spirit, two have explored the Spirit's work in the world today with faithfulness to the biblical revelation and with refreshing originality.

Joe Fison was nicknamed "the Prophet" by his contemporaries, and there is much of the prophet in his provocative book *Fire upon the Earth*. He identifies the story of the Holy Spirit's activity in a host of unexpected places.

> It would be churlish to deny something of true pro-phetic zeal and enthusiasm in such communist or near-communist community experiments as have been one of the most significant features of the rise to independence of the modern Israeli State . . . When anyone like David Low, the British cartoonist, or Diego Rivera the Mexican painter, or even Picasso, is speaking in any way on a burning contemporary issue, it is possible that he may be a prophet. If he is speaking at great personal sacrifice to himself, it is more than possible that he may be a true prophet.[2]

We may disagree with some of his identifications; but they kindle the imagination. If Fison can see God at work somewhere, it is more than possible (as he himself would say) that he is right. Whether in the light of subsequent events he would change his opinion, it is impossible to say.

Sometimes Fison is infuriatingly challenging to our ingrown patterns of thought, as in this passage on nationalism:

> In the light of the Biblical evidence, where are we likely to find the fire of revival "upon the earth" today? "Our

God is a consuming fire" (Hebrews 12:29) sounds
more like Zeta and nuclear energy than a cathedral
service or a prayer meeting! In view of the close connection in the Old Testament between the fire of the
primitive Spirit and the rise of Jewish nationalism, and
in view of the experiment in communism in the New
Testament immediately after Pentecost, the obvious
place to begin our search is in the contemporary nation-
alist and communist movements in the world today . . .
There is fire in the fanatical supporters of apartheid as
well as in the defense of the Johannesburg treason trial.
The deepest tragedy of Africa is that the fire that we hate
with a fiery hatred may be the very fire of which we are
most in need.[3]

John V. Taylor is less provocative, but just as intriguing, in
his exploration of the Holy Spirit in *The Go-Between God*.[4]
Unlike Fison, Taylor does not range widely through the world,
lighting almost randomly on things that seem to bear God's
touch. But like Fison he expects to find that touch everywhere.
He sees the Holy Spirit first in the flashes of recognition that
"change our minds and change our lives,"[5] that "turn an it into
a thou"[6] — the elusive force that defies definition and vanishes
when we try to focus on God, but gives meaning to people and
to actions. It would probably be true to Taylor's ideas to say that
wherever there is true meaning, it is God's story being written
on our lives.

He suggests three marks by which we can recognize the
Spirit's work: awareness, choice, sacrifice. He closes a chapter
by writing,

To make this concrete let me give three thumb-nail sketches.

"One thing I advise you to do," said the organization and method man to the management of a chain of city snack-bars, "is to rebuild all your lunch counters on a curve. It will cost you a lot initially, but at a straight counter every customer eats by himself and broods over his troubles. Experiments have shown that if you make them curved even the loneliest man will find himself talking to his neighbor." After a long tussle the organization man got his way.

In 1964 the Council of Churches in Rochester, New York, voted to donate 100,000 dollars to a militant community organization among poor blacks, despite the local radio station's decision to cancel the council's weekly religious program if it did so. It was a choice between an evangelism of action and an evangelism of words.

"I am afraid I have to tell you, doctor," said the ward sister, "that I am not prepared to follow your instructions in this case. I intend to let this patient know that she is dying. She's got it in her to rise to this, and I'll not rob her of her dignity."

In each of these three cases it is easy to identify the three characteristics of the Creator Spirit — the enhanced awareness, the necessity to choose and the "little death" of sacrifice. In each example I selected, the Spirit worked through Christians, but it need not be so, for the church depends on the Spirit, not the Spirit on the church. Even when the three clues mentioned above are given, it is possible to miss seeing the Spirit if you

have any preconceived ideas, for God may be working
at a carpenter's bench.[7]

Taylor's three tests — "awareness, choice, sacrifice" — are not
enough by themselves to recognize the Spirit of God. We
should need to add such words as "goodness", "healing," or
even "holiness," for he is known preeminently as the *Holy
Spirit*. But if Taylor's and Fison's accounts of the Spirit are true,
then any story with these characteristics can be read as the story
of God the Spirit, whether or not he is mentioned. And this is
hardly surprising, for Taylor himself describes the Spirit as God
working anonymously and on the inside: "the beyond in the
midst."[9]

[1] Justin, *Apology*, II, xiii; quoted in *Documents of the Christian Church*, edited
by Henry Bettenson (London: Oxford University Press, 1943), 7.

[2] J.E. Fison, *Fire upon the Earth* (London: Edinburgh House Press, 1958),
p.24-25.

[3] Ibid., 7.

[4] John V. Taylor, *The Go-Between God: The Holy Spirit and the Christian
Mission* (London: S.C.M. Press, 1972).

[5] Ibid., 16.

[6] Ibid., 17.

[7] Ibid., 40.

[8] Ibid., 5.

PART V

GOD'S STORY
IN OTHER PLACES

Chapter 16

The Creation

God's story is found in the Bible and found outside the Bible. That is to say, the Bible narrative is the touchstone by which we can test all of history, all of our personal lives, and through which we can recognize God's activity in both, but it is not by any means the only place where God is active. We should expect to find the motifs found in the Bible running through our own twentieth century. A look at four of these motifs, *the creation, the nation, the Christ, and the community*, explores ways in which modern writers are retelling these elements of God's story.

Creation is the obvious start. The first words of the Bible are about God's creating heaven and earth, and the last chapter of the Bible is about the new creation. In between, the whole book treats the world as God's world. The Bible is not an abstruse philosophical dissertation: it is centered in earthly things. The underlying assumption is that this world is the pattern of heaven. Jesus spoke of salt and bread, of sheep-rearing and planting and fishing, as if these bore the same divine imprint as the abiding realities of truth and love and joy. He made the common things of the physical world vehicles of his parables and allegories.

But the pattern of heaven is not heaven itself. We are not to expect this world to last forever. There is to be a destruction of what we know, and a new beginning. Because we cannot see in advance what this new beginning will be like, there is endless speculation about its timing, about its literal or metaphorical meaning, about its details or its broad panorama, but of one thing there can be no doubt: a new creation is promised in the Bible.

In our own generation creation and destruction and re-creation have taken on a new significance. Phrases like "space-ship earth," "endangered species," "global village" have become clichés. Photographs from space give us a chance to see our "floating ball" in a truer perspective. The first two nuclear bombs to be exploded on Hiroshima and Nagasaki have hammered into our minds the realization that life on this planet is very precarious. Perhaps we are on the brink of the prophesied destruction. Perhaps the new creation is about to be born.

This is clearly suggested by the researches of the "Club of Rome." In their study, *The Limits to Growth*[1] they state bluntly that there are five interlocking areas which are expanding very rapidly. They warn that unless a brake can be applied, we have perhaps a century left before disaster strikes. These five areas are: population growth, industrialization, agricultural production, depletion of natural resources, and pollution. Any one of these affects the others. Population growth, for example, compels higher agricultural production, for everyone must eat; it requires more industrialization to supply income for the higher population, which in turn depletes natural resources and often results in pollution.

The members of the "Club of Rome" are not fiction writers or visionaries, but businessmen, heads of corporations, researchers, whose stake in the future is as great as anyone's. Their conclusions are challenged; some regard them as alarmist pessimists. Millions of people, however, with less intellectual ability,feel in their bones that disaster is in the air. Two kinds of literature have brought into focus this sense that creation is reaching a climax: prophetic hypotheses and science fiction.

Hal Lindsay's book *The Late Great Planet Earth*[2] is not fiction, despite the possibilities implicit in its title. Lindsay examines in detail a number of predictions from various parts of the Bible, and fits them together to form a collage of future history. As he describes it, it is all very logical, if somewhat amazing. Lindsay is one of many Christians, over many centuries, who have taken biblical prophecy so literally that they have attempted to write the story of the future. Whether he has rightly interpreted the meaning of the original writers, and, more importantly, God's meaning of, is a matter of opinion until the future proves him right or wrong. And history has moved inexorably on since the book's publication in 1970. Whether he has rightly interpreted the meaning of the biblical writers, and, more importantly, God's meaning, is a matter of opinion until the future proves him right or wrong. And history has moved inexorably on since the book's publication in 1970.

Russia, he tells us, will one day attack a strong and prosperous Israel, and in turn be attacked and destroyed by a coalition of European states, a revival of the old Roman Empire in modern form, under a super-dictator. This "Future Fuhrer" is allied to a super-religion, a hybrid between degenerate Christian churches and occult worship. A Pan-Arab union, a pan-African union, and an immense army from China will all be involved in this, the last of all wars, at Megiddo, or Armageddon. But before this happens, those who truly believe in Jesus Christ will vanish, lifted bodily from the earth to be with him.

Here Lindsay does use fiction when he imagines the confusion that is left behind.

> There I was, driving down the freeway and all of a sudden the place went crazy . . . cars going in all directions . . . and not one of them had a driver!

> It was puzzling — very puzzling. I was teaching my course in the Philosophy of Religion when all of a sudden three of my students vanished. They simply vanished!

> My dear friends in the congregation. Bless you for coming to church today. I know that many of you have lost loved ones in this unusual disappearance of so many people . . . .[3]

Lindsay's point, of course, is that creation as we know it is only part of God's whole purpose. There is a further creation to come. History in this world will end (in a way predicted in the Bible) and the history of the next world — the history of eternity, if we can so express it — will ensue.

Arthur Clarke has no such loyalty to Scripture in *Childhood's End*.[4] Yet, like Lindsay, he reads the signs of the times and describes, this time openly in fiction, the next stage in Creation. To quote from his prologue:

> This was the moment when history held its breath, and
> the present sheared asunder from the past as an iceberg
> splits from its frozen, parent cliffs, and goes sailing out
> to sea in its lonely pride. All that the past ages had
> achieved was as nothing now: only one thought echoed
> and re-echoed through Reinhold's brain: the human
> race was no longer alone.[5]

Here again we are at the end of present history, and on the
verge of moving on to something as yet unknown. Some motifs
are surprisingly like those of prophecy, but treated in such a
different way that at first sight they are hardly recognizable.

> Karellen, the being from outer space who takes
> command of the whole earth (the "super-dictator"
> again) institutes an era of peace and prosperity such
> as has never been known. Only a few rebellious spir-
> its sense that freedom and creativity are being stifled.
> For a long time Karellen and his fellow overlords re-
> main out of sight in their giant spaceship, until they
> earn enough trust to reveal their true identity without
> imposing too much of a shock on humanity. They
> are, in fact, what we are accustomed to call "devils."
> Their mission, however, from the Overmind that con-
> trols them, is not to tempt but to act as midwives as
> humanity is born to its next stage.
>
> The time becomes ripe for the Overmind to
> achieve "Total Breakthrough" — that is, direct contact
> with a human mind. It starts with one child, who in
> his dreams travels deeper and deeper into space. His
> baby sister begins wielding mental control over her
> toys, and even absorbing food from the freezer with-

out the need to eat. Then, like an epidemic, this strange mental or spiritual energy takes control of children the world over. The Overlords evacuate them to a remote area where hundreds of millions of children, oblivious to their physical surroundings, absorb the energy of the earth and ultimately destroy it, having themselves merged into one super-conscious mind. Like a fiery cloud they trail off to meet, and perhaps be lost in, the Overmind.

The improbable ending is the logical outcome of a plot that many would regard as equally improbable. But Clarke's skill as a narrator enables his readers to imagine themselves in the situations that he describes, and the result may well be to ask oneself: "What then *is* the destiny of this planet? Is it to be dissolved as Clarke describes? Might the prophecies in the Bible be literally fulfilled? According to one such forecast, 'The heavens will disappear with a roar; the elements will be destroyed by fire . . .But in keeping with his promise we are looking forward to a new heaven and a new earth."[6] Is this any less improbable. What *will* be the end of creation?

[1] *The Limits to Growth*: the first phase of the Club of Rome's Project on the Predicament of Mankind, Survey of International Development, Vol. IX, No. 3 (March 1972).

[2] Hal Lindsay with C.C. Carlson *The Late Great Planet Earth* (Grand Rapids, Michigan: Zondervan Publishing House, 1970).

[3] Ibid. p. 136.

[4] Arthur C. Clarke, *Childhood's End* (New York: Ballantine Books. Toronto: Ballantine Books of Canada, 1953).

[5] Ibid., Introduction.

[6] II Peter 3:10,13.

Chapter 17

The Nation

"Israel is my firstborn son," said God.[1] "Salvation is from the Jews," added Jesus.[2] In the last book of the Bible is a vision of a hundred and forty-four thousand Israelites sealed with the seal of God on their foreheads.[3]

We cannot get away from the nation of Israel in the Bible. From start to finish these "Chosen People" dominate the story. Sometimes it looks as if God is not interested in anyone else.

The first few chapters of Genesis are merely the prelude, the setting, into which steps Abraham, the father of faith. Even Abraham gains part of his fame from being the grandfather of Jacob, whose name was changed to Israel.

Then comes the book of Exodus, and the drama begins to unfold. Israel's descendants are no more than a ghetto of slaves, but to God they are the core of history. God sends Moses, extensively trained and complete with miraculous power, to evacuate the slaves and to weld them into a nation. At Mount Sinai God gives them a constitution, based on the exclusive relationship between God and themselves. After Joshua leads them into the Promised Land, they ought to live an ideal life, obedient to God's commands, and enjoying God's protection.

But their politics and society deteriorate to the point where they need a monarchy to rule them and prophets to recall them to righteousness. For centuries their fortunes wax and wane, tending toward rebellion and failure. The rising dictatorships of the East finally catch up with them and the nation is demolished. Through it all, there runs the certainty that they are God's Chosen People. Even the disaster of the Babylonian exile is seen as God's punishment and, as such, not permanent. A minority return from Babylon to their given land, maintaining what little independence they can under the changing dictatorships. It is into this situation that Jesus is born.

From here, the national history diverges into two different streams. The sack of Jerusalem in 70 A.D. was a watershed in the story of Israel, an apparent end to their hopes. But the New Testament sees Jesus as the purpose and fulfillment of the national destiny. Rejecting him, the nation of Israel has forfeited its inheritance as the Chosen People. That title has gone to the international society of those who believe in Jesus as the Messiah.[4]

But is this really so? God never goes back on a promise. Israel has never been obliterated and the New Testament itself looks forward to their national restoration. St. Paul, in fact, speaks of Christians not so much superseding the Jews as being admitted to the privileges of their inheritance.

And that brings us to the present day. Israel has lost neither its identity nor its sense of destiny during the long years of dispersion. In this century the nation has returned, at least in part, to the Promised Land. There are those who see in this a violation of international law. There are those who see in it the keeping of a promise by God.

It would be easy to regard the return to the Promised Land as the twentieth century parallel to the motif of *nation* in God's story. Yet Israel is not the only nation in which God takes an interest, in spite of appearances to the contrary. There are hints of this even in the Bible. According to Amos, God brought up Israel out of the land of Egypt, and the Philistines from Caphtor, and the Syrians from Kir.[5] There may be no nation that fully parallels Israel's vocation, for Israel is the nation of Jesus, the unique Son of God. But every nation comes within the sphere of God's supervision.

Any perceptive telling of history is, in a sense, an account of God at work within one or more nations. As "King of kings and Lord of lords"[6] Jesus Christ continues his incarnation in history and in individuals. Our century has witnessed not only the great wars, but movements of nations that could well be described as miracles. For example, the independence of India and its continued friendship with its former British overlords; and more recently the demolition of the Berlin Wall and the evaporation of the Iron Curtain. In a television interview in Canada, Archbishop Desmond Tutu expressed the amazement of the world that F.W. de Klerk, President of South Africa, conferred with Nelson Mandela, who was jailed for so many years as leader of the banned African National Congress. Tutu's comment was: "As a Christian I can only say, 'There's a God around!'"[7]

If we turn to the southern United States we can find God at work there. A starting point is the novel *Roots*[8] by Alex Haley.

In a village in West Africa a young Mandinka warrior, fresh from his initiation into manhood, is captured by slave traders, and subjected to all the horrors and indignities of the ocean voyage and the auction. His lifetime of servitude is not without an attempt to escape. During his recapture he has one foot deliberately maimed. After his happy marriage and his apparent acceptance of his position, his only daughter is sold to another owner far more cruel than his own. Generation after generation, Haley traces the family until one of their descendants wins his freedom and settles on the land he has purchased.

The novel is a true one — true, that is, in the sense that the fiction is woven around established facts. Haley spent twelve years in researching his own origins. He claims descent from the Mandinka, Kunta Kinte. The hope of freedom that was kept alive from parent to child in the most trying times has emerged into a plea for genuine friendship between black and white, a plea perhaps the stronger for being only implicit in the story. Afro-Americans are not God's chosen people in the way that the Bible describes Israel; but they are God's people. They have neither more nor less claim on God than their white counterparts, unless suffering is a claim. It is as "Suffering Servant" that Israel found its finest vocation, and it is by the cross that Christ came to his resurrection. *Roots* is the story of the passion and resurrection of half a nation and it is a story that is still being told. The tragedy has not been completed yet and the triumph is only partially here. James Cone, in *Black Theology and Black Power*,[9] claims dogmatically that the only place where Christ can be found today is among the black folk.

The white church is apostate, he tells us. The deliberate shock of this assertion is softened when he defines "black" as the sufferers and "white" as the oppressors, and allows that whites who fully identify with the under-dog are really black.

For the news-watcher with open eyes, the story of God is written all the time in nations across the globe. It is for news reporters and novelists, historians and gossipers to identify what God is doing with the many chosen peoples.

[1] Exodus 4:22.

[2] John 4:22.

[3] Revelation 7.

[4] Romans 9-11.

[5] Amos 9:7.

[6] Revelation 17:14; 19:16.

[7] Canadian Broadcasting Corporation, "Journal," August 17, 1990.

[8] Alex Haley, *Roots* (Garden City, New York: Doubleday & Company, Inc. 1976).

[9] James Cone, *Black Theology and Black Power* (New York: Seabury Press, 1969).

Chapter 18

The Christ

The Bible is the story of a person, Jesus the Christ. He is the expectation of the Old Testament and the hero of the New Testament. For Christians, all of history is the preparation and the extension and the fulfillment of his story. The story of Jesus is, at least to our human experience, the focal point of God's story, and as such it is unique.

Look from a different angle, not at Jesus the Son of God, but at Jesus as Son of Man (which means, among other things, "human being"). Look at other people whose lives parallel his. Without denying that there are overtones in his story that can have no parallel, we can expect his character to be echoed in other characters. His achievements can be hinted at in the achievements of others, whether or not they acknowledge Jesus as their inspiration.

Two novels, out of the myriad possible, typify God's activity in ordinary folk in such a way that they resonate with the life of Jesus. Neither is factually true, although at least one claims to be based on an actual incident. Both of them have very simple

plots and this makes easy to analyze the mechanics behind
them.

The Exorcist[1] can be regarded as a truly Christian book. The
hysteria that greeted the film version should not blind us to the
novel's positive message: the title is not *The Devil-Possessed*, but
The Exorcist. The real hero is not the sick child, but the healer.
It is the story of healing at a heavy price, a price that reminds us
of the cross of Christ.

> A lonely young girl, through playing with a ouija
> board, allows herself to be invaded by another per-
> son. At first "he" seems to be a friend, but soon she
> undergoes a change of personality and becomes men-
> tally and physically ill. Medical help proves useless.
> At last an old priest is called in, a veteran of
> other battles with evil. He undertakes to exorcise the
> demon, assisted by a skeptical but willing younger
> priest. The ritual proceeds prosaically enough, but the
> strain proves too much for the older man's heart and
> he dies. The climax occurs when the young priest, left
> alone with the patient, suddenly is heard speaking in
> the deep voice that the demon uses. He leaps through
> the window to his death — and his own release from
> evil. Two men give their lives so that the little girl
> could be well again.

Inevitably any reader familiar with the Gospels recalls the
Gadarene swine, when the demons that "possessed" a human
being migrated at Jesus' command into a herd of pigs and
destroyed them.[2] A little more reflection brings to mind Paul's
phrase: "God made him who had no sin to be sin for us, so
that in him we might become the righteousness of God."[3] A

transfer takes place between the tormented and the healer; the healer has taken on himself the torment to free the victim.

Edgar Allen[4] is a less well-known tale of an American minister's family. It is told by the twelve-year-old son who describes the arrival of a small black boy for adoption.

>   The family's reaction is varied. Sally Ann and Stephen accept "E.A." with the naive friendship of little ones. Mary Nell, at fourteen, rejects him outright, and Michael, the narrator, finds himself forced to make a decision. His crisis comes when a schoolmate taunts him as a "nigger-lover." He replies, after a moment's pause, "Yes, he's my brother, Edgar Allen."[5]
>   The response of the all-white community is predictable. First there are polite stares, then a feeling of isolation, a hint that the minister should leave the parish, and at last a cross burnt on the lawn. The minister's reaction is predictable, too. He and his family must fight it out, however much they are hurt. Theirs will be an example to the community that will play its part in healing the nation's wounds. But — and here is the tragedy — the pressure proves just too much. After an incident that is the nearest the parents have ever come to a quarrel, E.A. is returned to the orphanage.
>   The minister's children are told that E.A.'s original parents have been found. Once this lie is exposed, Father is discredited both in his children's eyes and in those of the church. The book ends as he tries to rebuild the shattered trust of the family and prepares to look for a new parish.

All the characters in this story are well-drawn, but none so much as the gentle, sincere man who fails in his greatest crisis. He is a Christ-figure who makes the wrong choice. The Cross is too heavy to carry all the way. It is Mother then who is the healer, confronting young Michael with the need to bend, to accept, to forgive.

Both these books are worth reading, not only for their own sake, but as a lens through which to focus on the human story of Jesus. They reveal the cost at which He accepted the exorcism of the world and the possibility that He might have failed in one of His temptations. They are fictitious chapters in the true story of God.

Another facet of Jesus' life and death is paralleled in a true narrative from India. It concerns a young man named Jambulingam, known as "Raj" in the account by Amy Carmichael retold by Frank Houghton in *Amy Carmichael of Dohnavur*.[6]

> Raj, driven from his home by a false accusation and by fear of the police, has taken to a life of banditry in the hills, and is feared throughout South India as "The Red Tiger." But concern for the safety of his wife and children leads him to seek out an English Christian who is running an orphanage. She in turn leads him to put his trust in Jesus Christ.
>
> At this woman's urging he gives himself up, in the assurance of a fair trial and a light sentence. Instead, he receives torture and his leg is broken by a rifle butt. But his new found faith comes to his aid in an unexpected way. A clergyman reads to him from the Book of Acts the account of Peter's release from prison; and Raj is amazed one day to find his prison door open and unguarded. He seizes his opportunity

and escapes to the hills again. Now he no longer robs
or threatens travelers; he only "requests" money from
the rich, with which he helps the poor in the villages,
like a modern day Robin Hood. The word is out,
however, that the Red Tiger has escaped. Criminals
using his name terrorize the countryside, and build
up for him a reputation worse than before.

Betrayed by a supposed friend, Raj runs from the
police, but, hampered by his lame leg, he is cornered.
"He took cover, and fired one or two more shots to
delay the pursuit . . . Then suddenly he drew himself
up, sprang on to a bank of red earth, and threw his
gun away . . . He looked up to heaven, raised his
hands in worship, and then walked slowly back-
wards, and stood under a tamarind tree. Then the
police were upon him . . . "[7]

Here again is "obedience unto death."[8] Here is the Christ
portrayed in the life and death of a most unusual follower. Such
examples can be multiplied in the annals of the Christian
Church. They are the stories of Christians; they are the story of
Jesus; they are the story of God.

[1] William Blatty, The Exorcist (New York: Harper & Row Pubs., Inc., 1971).

[2] Mark 5:1-20 and parallels.

[3] 2 Corinthians 5:21.

[4] John Neufeld, Edgar Allen (New York: S.G. Phillips, Inc., 1968).

[5] Ibid., p. 57.

[6] Frank Houghton, Amy Carmichael of Dohnavur (London: S.P.C.K. 1953).

[7] Ibid., 133.

[8] Philippians 2:8.

Chapter 19

The Community

There is an ambiguity between the Kingdom of God and the Church. Jesus came to set up the Kingdom of God; he succeeded by leaving behind him the Church; yet the two are different.

C.H. Dodd, in his book *The Parables of the Kingdom*,[1] helped define the Kingdom of God, not as a realm with boundaries, not even as a society with exclusive membership, but as God's rule. In Jewish usage contemporary with the Gospels, to submit oneself unquestioningly to the Law is to "take upon oneself the Malkuth of heaven (i.e., kingdom of heaven)." In this sense the Kingdom of God is a present fact, but in another sense the Kingdom of God is something yet to be revealed.[2] Between the two is the ever-spreading community of those who belong to this kingdom. The New Testament, short as it is, concentrates upon the spreading of the Church — the community of God's people, but its mandate is to bring community wherever that rule touches. Its prayer, "Thy Kingdom come!" has many layers of fulfillment.

Anyone who sets out to tell the story of God's community is faced with this ambiguity: it is both the story of the Church and the story of the spread of liberation, of righteousness, of community. The two are not always the same.

Morris West capture an incident in the life of "the community" in *The Shoes of the Fisherman.*[3]

> The Pope is dead and a new pope must be elected. The stalemate between different factions is solved by the unexpected choice of a man who served many years in Soviet prisons. Bringing with him a new perspective, he begins a process of loosening old bigotries, both within the Vatican and on the international scene. Inevitably he has his opponents; he is less worried by them than by the emotional sickness and doubts that periodically overwhelm him. These weaknesses we are allowed to see through his private diaries.

In many respects this work of fiction has proved prophetic. Pope John XXIII, by convening the Second Vatican Council, began a loosening process very like that described in the novel. Pope John Paul II came from behind the Iron Curtain, and has thereby changed the political tensions of the world. Morris West probably does not have an inside knowledge of God's plans for ecclesiastical history, but he succeeds in describing God at work in the Roman Catholic Church and in the world at large.

A different moment, and a different spirit, is captured by Charles Kingsley in *Westward Ho!*[4] This sets out to be an adventure story, not a church story. It begins in the England of Elizabethan times and traverses the Atlantic and the new Spanish territories in America. It reflects the struggle between the Papacy and the Protestants, between despotism and freedom in half of Europe and the whole of future America. Which does God choose to be the law of the land?

> Amyas Leigh, a youngster brought up in the sea-faring tradition of Devonshire, is one of the party that sails round the world with Sir Francis Drake. Amyas first finds himself fighting the Spaniards who have invaded Ireland. Then, by a supreme irony, a Spanish officer he has taken prisoner elopes with the girl for whose hand he and several of his friends had established a friendly rivalry.
>
> Amyas equips an expedition to find her and sails for the Americas. He returns home with wealth captured from the Spaniards, but learns that his raid on the girl's home caused her, and his own captured brother, to be burnt at the stake. The "villain" who engineered this tragedy is none other than Amyas' own cousin, Eustace, who has been intriguing to bring back Catholicism to England.

Throughout the narrative there runs a thread of hatred not only between the two warring nations, but between two branches of the Church. On one side is the Roman Catholic Church, with the casuistry of the Jesuits, the tortures of the Inquisition, and the arrogant division of the world between Spain and Portugal; and on the other is the established Church of England, reformed but not pietistic, tolerant but strongly patriotic, and commanding an allegiance all but universal among the English.

To the twentieth century reader, with a climate of pluralism and a movement toward church unity, the picture drawn here has some very black patches. Whether Kingsley succeeds in telling historical truth, or whether his personal views color the story unwarrantably, he consistently tests the actions and the factions by their loyalty to the Gospel. There are serious faults among his English fighters, and there are saints among his Spanish Catholics. He does not identify the "kingdom" with either branch of the church: God's rule is obeyed (and disobeyed) in both.

But why limit the story to the church? God's activity is visible today not only in evangelism and church renewal, but in all movements toward freedom and justice that are budding and bearing fruit. The women's liberations movement, the toleration of other faiths, the increasing emphasis on freedom from want, these are symptoms of hope, and all are part of God's story.

So is the growing movement, in many parts of the globe, towards freedom from oppression by nations and societies. Mohandas K. Gandhi stands as a beacon in the story of God's community. Gandhi's biography has been written many times. The public's imagination was caught, however, by the film *Gandhi*, in which Ben Kingsley portrayed the title role.[4]

Foreshortened and simplified as the facts inevitably are, the film gives a clear account of the progress of India from British Imperial rule to its independence as a nation.

Mohandas Gandhi, a young Indian lawyer from London, arrives in South Africa to represent a client. He is amazed and enraged to be thrown out of a first class railway carriage because of his color. He sets out systematically to fight the law by which "coloreds" have to carry passes. Jailed with hundreds of his supporters, he is summoned to Prime Minister Jan Smuts' office to be told that he has won his immediate object, the repeal of the pass laws.

Later, back in India, he is recruited by men who have the independence of the country as their aim, Patel, Nehru, Jinnah and others. He tours India to discover that his country groans under oppressions he had not imagined. With the same tactics he used in South Africa, he fights the British government, defying the salt tax, the import of cotton cloth that is crippling Indian manufacture, and the cruelties, petty or flagrant, that he meets. Unfortunately, by the time he is called to take part in a constitutional conference for his country's independence, Jinnah has broken with him and campaigned for a separate Muslim state.

The terrible inter-religious slaughter that follows the partition of India and Pakistan is as abhorrent to Gandhi as the evils he has been fighting in imperialism. He declares that he will fast until the fighting ceases. Lying in a Muslim home in Calcutta, almost too weak to speak, he maintains his rigorous self-discipline until he is assured that a week has passed without bloodshed.

So the man who led the struggle for community between white and colored, between conqueror and conquered, between Hindu and Muslim, wins. He is the recognized idol of his compatriots, sainted in his lifetime. Huge crowds wait for him to appear for his daily prayer meeting, and among them is one with a gun. Gandhi is shot dead.

Here, no less than in church history, is God at work building community. If Gandhi never took the name of Christian, he took on himself the Kingdom of God. Like Jesus, it cost him his life. Gandhi is, both in his character and in his death, a Christ-figure. *The Calcutta Statesman*, in its editorial after Gandhi's death, could find no higher compliment for him than to compare him with Jesus.

Perhaps this analysis of the four biblical strands — creation, nation, Christ and community — is rather artificial, for all are part of the one story, the story of God. You can find God everywhere, in biography, history or fiction. You only need eyes that are open and a growing understanding of God.

[1] C.H. Dodd, *The Parables of the Kingdom* (London: Nisbet & Co., Ltd., 1935; 2nd printing, revised 1936).

[2] Ibid., 35-36.

[3] Morris L. West, *The Shoes of the Fisherman, A Novel* (New York: Morrow, 1963).

[4] Charles Kingsley, *Westward Ho!* (Cutchogue, New York: Buccaneer Books, 1982).

[5] *Gandhi*, Columbia Pictures, 1983.

PART VI

TELLING GOD'S STORY

Chapter 20

Bible Stories

So you want to try your hand at telling this wonderful tale, the story of God at work in the world?

Most likely you are already doing so, or you would not have read this far. Not many of us are writers, and even fewer are film producers, but there are legions of faithful men and women who preach the Gospel, teach in Sunday schools, entertain at camp fires . . . . Each of these occupations requires a fund of stories to be told and retold with freshness.

Probably the most frequent and powerful form of story for the preacher (by this I mean all who communicate Christ by word of mouth) is the biblical story. II Timothy 3:16 is almost a platitude for preachers: "All scripture is God-breathed and is useful for teaching . . ."

There is a world of difference between reading the Bible aloud and retelling it in your own words. Retelling it is not a substitute for reading it. The actual words of Scripture often prove to have a power in themselves, a power that is as mysterious and indefinable as it is effective.

J.B. Phillips, in his preface to *Letters to Young Churches*, wrote:

> The present translator . . . without holding
> fundamentalist views of 'inspiration,' . . . is continually
> struck by the living quality of the material on which he
> is working . . . again and again the writer has felt rather
> like an electrician rewiring an ancient house without
> being able to 'turn the mains off.'[1]

Moreover, whether or not you are convinced that the written Word itself has power, the regular use of it in public helps to develop a respect among the listeners, and tends to etch it indelibly on the listener's memory. But simply to read it, even in a modern form, may not grip the listeners in the way that a fresh telling does.

The story goes that Phillips himself wrote *Letters to Young Churches*, and subsequently paraphrased the rest of the New Testament, for the following reason. He was in an air raid shelter one evening during the Second World War. Londoners spent almost every night underground. Whole neighborhoods would meet in the shelters when the air raid siren sounded and sleep in communal dormitories. Noticing that a number of the young people of his parish were in the same shelter, Phillips called them together and read them a passage from the New Testament that seemed particularly appropriate to the apocalyptic days through which the nation was passing. He was met by polite indifference. "They haven't understood a word of it," he said to himself.

He spent the next day in his study with his Greek Testament, and by nightfall he had a manuscript prepared. Once again he invited his young parishioners to listen to him.

"You didn't understand what I was reading last night, did you? Now listen to this." The listeners' eyes lit up. "Coo, that's what's happening right now, isn't it, Sir?" they said. "Yes, you're right," he replied. "But do you realize that what I read you tonight is exactly the same as I read yesterday, only I put it into language that you could understand?"

In the introduction to this book, C.S. Lewis agrees with Phillips' estimate that the accurate transmission of the Word of God does not depend on an archaic translation. To Lewis, the use of the current vernacular, however vulgar or utilitarian, was a direct reflection of the Incarnation.

> The New Testament in the original Greek is not a work of literary art . . . . The same divine humility which decreed that God should become a baby at a peasant-woman's breast, and later an arrested field-preacher in the hands of the Roman police, decreed also that He should be preached in a vulgar, prosaic and unliterary language . . . . We ought therefore to welcome all new translations (when they are made by sound scholars) and most certainly those who are approaching the Bible for the first time will be wise not to begin with the Authorized Version.[2]

What he says of new translations applies also to storytelling. For what is a "Bible story" except a translation of the Word of God into words that the listener can appreciate? Lewis' proviso that the translators be "sound scholars" could be interpreted to mean that storytellers be accurate as well as imaginative.

Another reason for the use of your own words is that the original narratives are so short. The writers were limited by the materials at their disposal. We, with our typewriters, printing presses, faxes and computers, find it hard to imagine not only writing a manuscript by hand, but transcribing by hand each successive copy. So the Gospel writers, for example, made no attempt to include the background descriptions that any modern novelist would consider essential. Their purpose was not to write a biography but to proclaim the Good News. When the pith of the story was clearly expressed, they had done their work. That is why the Gospel of Mark, with its sixteen short chapters, would fit into a single chapter of a writer today. The reading of the Gospel has to be supplemented with exposition — and filled out into a story.

This book cannot give you instruction on the technique of telling stories — the delivery, elocution, use of visual aids, and so on. It is concerned about the content. The most successful teller of stories, however, is also an actor. The narrator enters the story in imagination, so that words and actions come from the heart, not from rote.

The first thing when working with a biblical story is to read and reread the episode. Next meditate on it, until you can picture it actually happening. Find out, if you can, what sort of plants or animals might have been seen. Think of the geography of the area. When Jesus fed the five thousand with a handful of bread and fish,[3] was the setting sun in his eyes? How big do you think the basket was in which Paul was lowered over the city wall?[4] Which was worse: feeling foolish or feeling cramped?

Accuracy of geography or botany is relatively unimportant, unless it plays a part in the development of the plot. What matters is to understand what happened and why it happened. You are telling a story not merely to entertain. Remember Dorothy L. Sayers' rule, quoted in chapter 6, that a story must be told for its own sake, not to preach. Perhaps what she intended to say was that a story must be told with such integrity that the preaching is done by the telling. The preaching cannot come through a moral tacked on to the end, or by a false aura of sanctity that insulates Bible stories from real life. The Bible stories *are* real life.

There is no need to start where the original writer started. The repetition of the words of the Bible does not only imprint them on the memory; it can have a deadening effect. We need to be shocked out of our comatose habits of hearing without listening. Often it helps to take a different point of view. The story of the feeding of the five thousand[5] can be told from the view point of the boy whose dinner buns were borrowed by Jesus to feed the crowd; or the entry into Jerusalem[6] told as the donkey might have seen it. The crucifixion, that central fact of the whole Gospel, lends itself to all manner of different angles. One such might be as follows (expanded to whatever length the occasion demands):[7]

Barabbas lay on the stone floor of the jail, his arms sore from the iron chains with which he was fixed to the damp walls, his back throbbing from the whipping that the Roman guards had given him. [You may be shown in Jerusalem a room that was probably the jail in Jesus' day. Quite possibly both Barabbas and Jesus were incarcerated there for at least part of that fateful night.] He was hungry; he was worn out; but mostly he was furious. After months of preparation he had given the word to his followers to move in on Jerusalem and attack the Roman sentries, to rise in rebellion against the oppressive government, to throw the Romans out of the country and set up a Jewish state. Now here he was — a captive in a Roman dungeon, condemned to death as a rebel and a murderer.

Through the grating of his cell came the roar of the crowd. He could hear his name shouted again and again: "Barabbas! Barabbas." "The dirty wretches!" he muttered to himself. "I thought I could trust them. I thought the whole country would rise in arms when I gave the signal, and now there they are shouting against me!"

The roar grew louder, but the words were different. Barabbas strained his ears to hear. "Crucify him!" they were shouting; and again and again: "Crucify! Crucify!" In despair Barabbas sank down on the straw he had been given for a bed. Was that all that his fellow-citizens thought of him?

Suddenly he heard footsteps on the stairs, a key grated in the lock, and the door was flung open. A burly guard appeared, armed with a hammer and chisel. Without a word he knelt beside Barabbas to sever the chains on his wrists and ankles. Then he pulled him to his feet, and gave him a push toward the door. "Go on, get out," he said.

Barabbas was too stunned to move. "Why? What has happened?" he managed to blurt out. "They're crucifying that other man instead of you," the guard replied. "Get out of here! You don't deserve it. He's done nothing wrong, but he's dying instead of you."

Barabbas stumbled out into the sunshine, and followed the crowd out of the city. There he watched as Jesus, his fellow-prisoner of the previous night, was nailed to the cross. For the rest of that day — for the rest of his life — the jailer's words echoed in his conscience: "He's done nothing wrong, but he died instead of me!"

Short as it is, even this account would need to be expanded if it were told in public; but the kernel is there. The facts of the story have not been changed, except to expand them imaginatively and the impact of a statement such as "Christ died for the ungodly"[8] is maintained. Pär Lagerkvist has used the same story as a short novel, *Barabbas,*[9] in which he follows the former rebel leader's subsequent career, a career irrevocably altered by the man who died for him.

Any would-be speaker would do well to take an incident from the Bible and practice relating it from each different character's point of view. It can make the Bible live more vividly for you as well as for the hearers. The crucifixion narrative could be told from the point of view of Simon Peter, of John, of Pilot, of an unknown passer-by. It depends most of all on the depth to which you immerse your own imagination in the story. Once it is truly "yours," you will be able to relay it to others with freshness and power.

[1] J.B, Phillips. *Letters to Young Churches: A Translation of the New Testament Epistles,* with an introduction by C.S. Lewis (London: Geoffrey Bles, 1947), xii.

[2] Ibid., vii-viii.

[3] Mark 6:33-44 and synoptic parallels, also John 6:1-15.

[4] Acts 9:23-25; 2 Corinthians 11:32-33.

[5] John 6:1-15.

[6] Mark 11:1-11 and parallels, also John 12:12-19.

[7] Mark 15:6-15 and parallels, also John 18:38-19:6; but the whole crucifixion narrative needs to be studied in all four Gospels.

[8] Romans 5:6.

[9] Pär Lagerkvist, *Barabbas*, translated by Alan Blair, with a preface by Lucien Maury and a letter by Andre Gide (New York: Random House, 1951; paperback: Bantam edition, 1962).

Chapter 21

Types

Typology is a discredited science among many Bible scholars, which is a pity, for there is no doubt that the New Testament writers themselves employed it. The New Testament writers did not go to the same excesses of exegesis, however, as some more modern writers. A *type* is someone or something that has its own value in the Old Testament narrative, but is matched by a corresponding person or thing —usually some aspect of Jesus Christ — in the New Testament. C.I. Scofield defines it as

> . . . a divinely purposed illustration of some truth. It may be (1) a person (Rom. 5:14); (2) an event (I Cor. 10:11); (3) a thing (Heb. 10:20); (4) an institution (Heb. 9:11); (5) a ceremonial (I Cor. 5:7) . . . . The antitype, or fulfillment of the type, is found, usually, in the New Testament.[1]

A simpler description from the Concise Oxford Dictionary, is a "Biblical event regarded as symbolic or foreshadowing a later one."[2] Scofield makes great use of this method of reading the Old Testament and is guilty of some very questionable interpretations. For example, the same verse at which his definition of a type is given, Genesis 1:16, reads in the King James Version: "And God made two great lights; the greater light to rule the day, and the lesser light to rule the night: he made the stars also."

It is difficult to accept Scofield's thesis:

> The "greater light" is a type of Christ, the "Sun of Righteousness" (Mal. 4:2). He will take this character at His second advent. Morally the world is now in the state between Gen. 1:3 and 1:16 . . . The sun is not seen, but there is light . . . The stars (Gen. 1:16) are individual believers who are "lights" (Phil. 2:15,16). See John 1:5. [3]

It's doubtful that the Holy Spirit meant all that through the agency of the writer of Genesis, although undoubtedly some people have found inspiration in the idea. It spoils the flow of the narrative to be constantly looking for esoteric meanings in simple things.

And yet types there are aplenty. Many are explicitly given their meaning in the New Testament. The Letter to the Hebrews is *par excellence* a book of antitypes, interpreting the details of the Old Testament tabernacle and priesthood in terms of Christ.

For Christians one strong reason for reading — and recounting — the Old Testament stories can be that so many of them refer to Christ. Of course this is not their only meaning. The text has a validity for its own time and people, and the first rule in understanding any portion of the Bible is: What did it mean *when it was written?* But it appears as if God deliberately made history "rhyme"; an incident that took place hundreds of years before the Savior's incarnation is repeated, not exactly, but with sufficient closeness to take our breath away. One such episode is Passover, that rescue that is basic to the faith of the Jewish nation.[4]

> Into the ghetto of Israelites under the Egyptian dictatorship comes Moses, an Israelite himself, but with the upbringing of an Egyptian priest-prince and years of experience as a desert shepherd. With boundless confidence that he is God's spokesman, he orders all the people to hold a roast lamb banquet in their homes, first saving the blood of the slaughtered lambs and painting their door-frames with it. The purpose of these actions is to identify the homes of God's people. That night God will send death to all the unmarked homes in the land.
>
> The disaster strikes the Egyptians as promised and their king urgently dismisses the Israelites from his country for fear of worse consequences. So begins the journey through the Sinai Peninsula, and so begins the annual festival that is held the world over in celebration of freedom.

A.M. Hodgkin, in *Christ in All the Scriptures*,[5] details at least some possible interpretations of this event. He writes:

> With many of the types we feel that we may not have interpreted them rightly, but with some we can have no doubt, for God has told us the meaning. It is so in this case, and in most of the types of Exodus. *"Christ our*

Passover is sacrificed for us: therefore let us keep the feast" (I. Cor. v.7,8). . . . [6]

Exod. xii.6. It was a *slain* lamb — not a living one — that availed the Israelites in the hour of judgment.	1 Cor. ii.2. I determined not to know anything among you, save Jesus, and *Him crucified.*
Ver. 5. The lamb was to be without blemish. Ver. 7. Its blood was to be shed and applied to the doorposts.	1 Pet. i. 18, 19. Ye were . . . redeemed . . . with the precious blood of Christ, as of a lamb without blemish and without spot.
Ver. 46. No bone of it was to be broken.	John xix. 36. That the Scripture might be fulfilled, A bone of Him shall not be broken.
Ver. 3 and 20 *[sic; this is evidently a misprint; it should read ver. 3 and 30].* In *every* home that night there was one dead, either the firstborn or the lamb in the stead of the first-born.	Rom. vi. 23. The wages of sin is death. Rom. v. 8. While we were yet sinners Christ died for us. [7]

Again we might question some of the details of this interpretation; but clearly the New Testament writers regarded Passover as a type of the Christian's redemption. Indeed, it seems clear that Jesus himself so interpreted his own death, by the urgency with which he choose Passover as the time for his passion. [8]

And the Israelites' subsequent journey through the desert was clearly in Paul's mind when he taught of the Christian life in I Corinthians 10. Verse 11 of that chapter is as near as the Bible itself has to a definition of types: "These things happened to them as examples, and were written down as warnings for us, on whom the fulfillment of the ages has come."

So when you find yourself teaching the lives of the heroes and heroines of old, there may be more to them than merely ancient history, or even examples of faith.[9] Ask yourself, "Can I tell this story in such a way as to make Jesus more real to my listeners?" David and Goliath[10] is a favorite: but was Jesus a David facing the Goliath of evil? Or is the less familiar figure of Joshua[11] the High Priest, seen in a vision as having his dirty clothes replaced with his priestly regalia, a picture of Jesus returning to his glory after taking the sins of the world on himself?[12]

Two of the most striking parallels between Old and New Testaments occur in the Book of Genesis.

> Joseph was his father's favorite son (Jesus is his Father's only begotten Son). In spite of Joseph's certainty that one day he would receive great honor within family, his complete obedience leads him into disaster. Joseph narrowly escapes a lynching by his brothers, and finds himself a slave. Even then he has not reached rock bottom, for a false accusation lands him in prison. Some time later, he is "raised again"; he is "highly exalted" and set at the right hand of the King; he is given "a name which is above every name";[13] he became the savior not only of his adopted nation but of the entire ancient world.[14]

Did Paul have this story in mind when he wrote the great poem of Philippians 2: 6-11?

> Abraham had only one son (Ishmael was out of the picture by this time) whom he dearly loved (again the "only- begotten son," or the "beloved son" of Mark 1:11). For reasons that are beyond his understanding or ours, God told him to sacrifice that son. With heroic faith he trekked with him to the sacrificial mountain, where, at the very last moment, God prevented him from committing murder. It was without doubt by divine planning that at that very moment he noticed a ram trapped in the bushes, and this proved an acceptable substitute for his son.[15]

There are so many strands interwoven in this story that a Christian storyteller has to avoid confusing the audience with a profusion of antitypes. You can treat Abraham as a type of God the Father, and Isaac as the obedient Son of God, who went willingly to his death. The story appears in Hebrews 11:17-19 as a parable of resurrection. You can equally well see Jesus in the ram, offered as a substitute. We are all Isaacs, doomed to die, but spared by his death instead of ours.

Two warnings are needed when you are working with types. The first is that you cannot *prove* anything with them. They are excellent for devotion, but not for dogmatic theology. Where the New Testament gives the meaning, you are on safe ground; it is dangerous to go beyond that.

The other warning rises from that: if the antitype is not made clear in the Bible, beware! Perhaps the incident is not a valid type at all. Too easily we can teach as true ideas that were nurtured in our own imagination. This is not to say that it is never legitimate to find types in unlikely spots. They can be excellent sermon illustrations (of which more in the next chapter.) An example can be found in Esther. It has been pointed out that the Book of Esther does not once contain the name of God, but God is certainly present in the plot.

> A young Jewish girl finds herself chosen to be the chief queen in the harem of the Persian emperor. Her uncle, hearing of a plot to exterminate the Jews, warns her and begs her to ask her husband to prevent the slaughter. "Who knows but that you have come to royal position for such a time as this?"[15]
> Unfortunately, the emperor appears to have lost interest in her. Besides, to enter his presence uninvited means instant death — unless he holds out his royal scepter. Queen Esther, fully aware of this, goes to the throne room with her petition. The emperor extends his scepter in welcome and she saves her people.

The exposition in *Christ in All the Scriptures* reads:

> There have been various attempts to trace elaborate types in the Book of Esther, but the simple fact stands out that here was one who was willing to lay down her life for her people. It is here that we find Christ in the Book of Esther. A picture of Him who was not only willing, but who did lay down his life for us, through whose intercession salvation is assured to us.[16]

[1] *The Holy Bible . . .* edited by Rev. C.I. Scofield, D.D (Oxford University Press, American Branch, 1917) fn. to Genesis 1:16.

[2] *Concise Oxford Dictionary* (Oxford: Clarendon Press, 1964).

[3] Scofield, *Bible* fn. to Genesis 1:16.

[4] Exodus, passim, especially chapter 12.

[5] A.M. Hodgkin, *Christ in All the Scriptures* (London: Pickering & Inglis Ltd., 1907), 17.

[6] Other verses that imply the same thing include 1 Peter 1:18-19, Revelation 1:5.

[7] *Christ in All the Scriptures,* 17-18.

[8] e.g. Luke 22:15.

[9] Hebrews 11, passim.

[10] I Samuel 17.

[11] In God's plan it may not be an accident that the High Priest's name was Joshua, which, after translation into Greek and then into English, is the same as Jesus.

[12] Zechariah 3:1-7; I Peter 2:24.

[13] Genesis 41:43. The exact meaning of "Abrek" is unknown; it is translated in the *King James Version* as "Bow the knee!" and in the *Jerusalem Bible* as "Make way!" In any case it was an ascription of honor and authority.

[14] Genesis chapters 37 ff.

[15] Genesis 22: 1-14.

[16] Esther 4: 14

[17] *Christ in All the Scriptures,* 101.

Chapter 22

Illustrations

A theological student returned to his college in great excitement. "I've got three magnificent sermon illustrations," he announced. "Now all I need is a Bible verse to go with them!"

Perhaps that never happened; but it is itself an illustration of how *not* to use illustrations. Every preacher and every teacher knows that an unrelieved spate of statements or exhortations becomes boring. Short stories that illustrate the meaning of the message rekindle the attention, but they do more. They turn on a light in the mind, enabling the listener to grasp clearly what the speaker is trying to express; and they imprint it on the memory. Next to a visual aid, an appropriate story does more than anything else to help us remember what we hear. Probably this is because when a story is told well, we actually see it happening on the retina of our imagination. It becomes a surrogate visual aid. It is only an aid, however. It is not the story itself that is important, but the message.

The story must be an appropriate story, one that fits the theme and advances the argument, rather than distract from it.

Jesus was a master of the art of illustrations. In fact, his illustrations — we call most of them parables — survive in the communal memory far better than his other words. The crowds who flocked to hear him were not simply seeking the entertainment of a traveling storyteller: they were listening to the Good News of the Kingdom of God. Much of what he told them must have been lost. It is his stories that crystallized their understanding into memory, and so were recorded in the Gospels.

Some of his stories were as short as a few words, such as "By their fruits you will recognize them. Do people pick grapes from thornbushes, or figs from thistles?"[1] Some were cameos, crystal clear and utterly memorable, like the tales of the Hidden Treasure and the Valuable Pearl.[2] Others again were full stories — the Ten Bridesmaids,[3] the Good Samaritan,[4] the Prodigal Son.[5] Always he used scenes that were familiar; for it goes without saying that a story that itself has to be explained is not very successful in explaining a deeper reality.

Often his parables stood alone, without explanation, without a "moral." But frequently he put them into the context of his teaching by starting them with "The Kingdom of Heaven is like . . . ." Sometimes he followed a story with a challenge "Go and do likewise."[6] "Therefore keep watch..."[7]

Occasionally Jesus went out of his way to explain his meaning, as in the parables of the Sower and the Seed[8] and of the Tares.[9] But always it was not the story that was the core of his teaching, but its meaning. The story was no more and no less than an aid to understanding and to memory.

There is no reason why you should stick slavishly to the form of Jesus' parables. If it is legitimate to invent details in recounting a historical event, how much more legitimate in retelling fiction. It depends on the immediate aim. If you are teaching the Bible for its own sake — and a very laudable aim that is — then it is important to leave as accurate a memory as possible of the biblical words. But if you are using one of Jesus' parables as an illustration during an address, then it is appropriate to set it in the hearers' milieu.

In the parable of the Good Samaritan, why not have a driver mugged by a lonely road, and helped by a native Indian — or a black person — or a drug addict — or an AIDS sufferer, whichever is the local equivalent of the "Samaritan"? The authors of *Godspell*[10] intended both a laugh and a memory aid when, after Jesus' warning that lack of reconciliation might land you in jail, they quoted from the game of Monopoly: "Go directly to jail. Do not pass 'GO.' Do not collect $200."

Obviously illustrations do not have to come from the Bible. Here are three stories that I have heard used with telling effect, and that I have often repeated myself. All three have considerable detail; but notice how in each case there is a single point emphasized. The first illuminates the phrase in Acts 20:28, " . . . the church of God, which he bought with his own blood."

A boy [give him a name if you wish] set out to build himself a model yacht. He took enormous pains to make it accurate. Finally it was complete, with its spars, its rigging, its sails, and of course its name. Excitedly he took it down to the beach and launched it. It sailed beautifully — too beautifully. Imagine his dismay when a gust of wind took it out of

his reach, and he watched it disappear round a head-
land on the ebbing tide.

Some time later, he was browsing in a hobby
shop when he saw a yacht that looked exactly like his.
It was the same size, the same color — yes, it had the
same name. "Please," he said to the storekeeper,
"that's my boat! Can I have it?" "Sure, you can have
it — for $25. That's the marked price. What do you
mean, it's yours?" "Of course it's mine! I made it!" "I
don't know anything about that, but it's not yours
until you come up with the full price."

Week after week he saved his pocket money, and
frequently he returned to the store to make sure that
the boat was still unsold. At last he strode trium-
phantly to the counter and said, "There's the money!
Now may I have my boat?"

As he carried it home, he stroked the hull lov-
ingly, and said: "Now you are twice mine. I made you
— and I paid the price for you."

Why did Jesus have to die? Could God not have ignored
our sin, or at least found some easier way to forgive us? Did
even God have a problem like the following?

The chieftain of a small medieval country determined to put a stop to bribery. Calling his chief of
police, he instructed him to give the next person
caught offering or receiving a bribe a hundred strokes
of the cat-o'-nine-tails. "No one will be willing to face
that," he said, "and if one does, nobody else will."

One day the chief of police reported that he had
found someone accepting a bribe. "Well, you know
what to do," said the chieftain. "Yes, sir, but you

ought to know who it is." "I don't care who it is!" the chieftain exclaimed. "There is only one law for all: one hundred lashes of the cat!" "Very good, sir, but . . . " "All right, who is it?" "It's your mother, sir."

Now the chieftain was caught in a trap. If he administered the punishment, what sort of a son was he? And if he made an exception, what sort of a leader was he? Justice and love were at odds with each other. [And here, when telling this story, I usually add: "And that is exactly the quandary that God is in. God is perfect justice and perfect love . . . "]

All night he paced his room, and in the morning he called his chief of police. "Tie up the prisoner and begin," he said. The policeman brought down the whip once. "Now stop!" ordered the chieftain. "Untie her — and give me ninety-nine!" ["And the difference with Jesus is that he took the full hundred . . . "]

I do not know the author of either of these stories. A sermon illustration, once used, is hard to copyright. But I can vouch for the third one. Dick Rees, an Anglican minister who was once a chaplain in the British forces, said it happened to him. He used the story to point out that "evangelism" means "sharing good news."

He was stationed somewhere in the Middle East, when a parcel from England arrived, containing a large slab of his favorite candy, coconut ice. He was just licking his lips in anticipation of enjoying it, when he was called away on duty. He returned to find that the coconut ice had disappeared — all except for a tiny piece. Up one leg of the table, across the top and down the other leg moved a column of ants. Each one paused at the coconut ice, bit off a small piece, and took it away.

There must have been one ant in the tent when he opened the parcel. This ant had discovered the delicacy. But instead of keeping the secret to itself, it had gone back to its comrades and told them: "Good News! There's coconut ice free for the taking!"

The application is clear enough. But there is a further point to be garnered from this episode: namely, that if you keep your eyes open, all sorts of things can help you illustrate your faith. The one requirement is that you be so soaked in the Gospel that the illustration fits the message. If not, you might fall into the same trap as the theological student on the look-out for illustrations, but with no message.

[1] Matthew 7:16.

[2] Matthew 13:44-46.

[3] Matthew 25:1-13.

[4] Luke 10:30-37.

[5] Luke 15:11-32.

[6] Luke 10:37.

[7] Matthew 25:13.

[8] Matthew 13:3-9 and 18-23.

[9] Matthew 13:24-30 and 36-43.

[10] See Chapter 9, fn. 6.

PART VII

WRITING GOD'S STORY

Chapter 23

Biblical Novels

"Of making many books there is no end," wrote the author of Ecclesiastes.[1] Even he would be amazed if he could browse through a modern bookstore. And despite the many books published, there is always a call for more.

There must be thousands of unwritten novels and plays floating in the imagination of people too uncertain of themselves to put pen to paper and thousands more written and never published. Why not try your skill? If you have ideas in your head that you would like to share with the public, you will never succeed until you write them down. Admittedly, it is not easy to get them into print, but you will certainly not see them printed if you never write them.

Where do you start? You want to see God becoming visible in the pages you write, but how? If Part III of this book is true, God will come through anyhow. Everything you do and everything you say reflects something of what you believe about God.

But you want to be a little more deliberate in making God known. Is it possible to include God as an actor in your plot, without thereby reducing God to a fictional character? You might try your hand on a Biblical novel; but be careful: it's not easy.

Let me introduce you to the Inklings. They were a group of writers who used to meet regularly in Oxford to compare and discuss their writings and to encourage each other on the different paths they had chosen. Four members of this literary club come to mind, all Christian, all determined to tell God's story (though they might not have used that expression), and all fiction writers.

One in particular achieved outstanding success with a series of radio dramas, taken straight from the Gospels. Dorothy L. Sayers was already well-known for her detective fiction when she was commissioned to write *The Man Born to be King*.[2] In it she tells the story of Jesus as nearly as possible as his contemporaries might have seen him. Her account of her method is illuminating. The material, she writes, "should be handled, not liturgically or symbolically, but realistically and historically: 'this is a thing that actually happened.' "[3]

In the first of the series, she did consciously sacrifice realism to symbolism in her depiction of the three "kings" who came to Bethlehem, by maintaining their traditional names and places of origin and treating them with an air of religious mystery. In all the other plays, however, she made the characters as lifelike as possible, bearing in mind that she was writing for English children. "The technique is to keep the ancient setting, and to give the modern equivalent of the contemporary speech and manners."[4] She made Matthew a cockney and Judas Iscariot a university graduate. Jesus is seen not only in the spotlight of heaven, but in the footlights of some very human situations. For example, when someone asks him how his father is, he replies: "Joseph Ben-Heli rests in Abraham's bosom;" and Martha, fussing over the dinner, wants to know whether Jesus prefers fig stuffing or dates. How would we ever know? And does it matter? No, but the detail adds to the realism of the play.

Naturally there is much fiction involved, and Sayers reinforces the unity of the series by identifying several women throughout the Gospel as Mary Magdalene, and by rolling several centurions into one. Whether this illuminates the core of fact and so reveals "truth," or whether this distorts truth by altering fact, must remain a matter of subjective judgment.

Biblical narrative is difficult. The writer is walking a tightrope. On one side is the pull of faith. No one has a right to distort the material. A biblical novel differs from a historical novel, not in the accuracy of the facts that it deals with, but in the value set on those facts by the author and the readers.

For example, Shakespeare played fast and loose with Scottish history when he wrote *Macbeth*, and no one blames him for it. On the other hand, when Racine wrote *Athalie*, it appears that he took great pains to see that he remained true to the sacred text. You have to imagine the setting; you cannot avoid adding to the action, and if there is any dialogue at all, it is bound to be fictitious. But you dare not tamper with the meaning of the original. Most importantly, you dare not distort the person of Christ.

The main cause of the outcry against the film *The Last Temptation of Christ*, based on the novel of the same name by Nikos Kazantzakis[5] was that it distorted some people's image of Christ. It is a boldly imaginative account of the thoughts of Jesus as he hung on the cross. A whole lifetime passes in his

thoughts between the words, "My God, my God . . . " and
" . . . why have you forsaken me?"[6] With relief Jesus emerges
from his hallucination and realizes he has *not* come down
miraculously from the cross. He has, in fact, kept faith with his
Father. The Jesus of the film (and book) is not Jesus as most
Christians experience him, hence the outcry.

On the other side of the tightrope there is another trap: to
be so afraid of unfaithfulness to the text so as to be unoriginal.
You can fail to tell a good story for its own sake. A further
pitfall is the urge to moralize, to explain the allegory, to point
the meaning of the parable. A story is its own justification.

Three accounts of the life of David can illustrate this
difficulty. Duff Cooper, a British politician, wrote a book titled,
simply, *David*.[7] He skillfully disentangles David's political
motives, but he fails to grip the reader: no one is allowed to say
anything except through quotations from the Bible — the King
James Version at that. Cooper seems so afraid of changing the
meaning that he changes too little.

Frank Slaughter fails in the opposite direction in *David,
King and Warrior*.[8] The extra incidents that he invents (such as
David's first meeting with his future wife Michal) are credible
enough; but the certainty of a happy ending robs the book of
the resurrection quality that marks the story of God. Further,
Slaughter cannot resist the temptation to point out a moral
occasionally.

Laurene Chinn has kept a good balance in *The
Unanointed*.[9] The hero is Joab, the man who never quite
succeeds, the "unanointed" whose life is played out against the
successes of his royal cousin. King David's charismatic
leadership springs from a grimier character than that to which

we are accustomed. Chinn has stripped off much of the added tinsel of sacred tradition, and exposed the dirt beneath. The result is that we meet a very real and not always lovable man.

> David marries the girl whom Joab already loves. He makes Joab his best man at his wedding and he claims Joab's child, Amnon, as his own. David spoils the boy as he grows up, but unpredictably ignores his son on his birthday when politics claim his attention. No wonder Amnon is a cause of David's later worries!

Such weaknesses are evidence of sin at the core of David's personality, no less than is his adultery with Bathsheba. By the end of the book we have been told no morals, but we are driven to ask: "Was David really like that? What would I have done in his shoes — or in Joab's shoes?" Possibly also we shall have to ask: "Could it have been true that Amnon was indeed not David's own son? Is this a distortion of the Bible narrative, or an interpretation?"

So any incident in the Bible could be written into a short story, a play, or a novel. In essence the technique is the same as telling the story aloud, but it requires even more care. For errors of fact or interpretation that might be forgiven a speaker are certain to be noticed in a book. Imagination and faithfulness to the text need to be kept in a disciplined balance. The degree of faithfulness — or the liberties that one is prepared to take with it — would depend on both the writer's view of inspiration, and the view that the readers might be expected to take. For if the Bible is "Holy Writ," then a novel that sets out to tell God's story dare not contradict that story as it is already recorded there. It can expand, it can interpret, but it should never distort the original.

[1] Ecclesiastes 12:12.

[2] Dorothy L. Sayers, *The Man Born to be King*, A Play Cycle on the Life of Our Lord Jesus Christ (London: Victor Gollancz Ltd., 1943).

[3] Ibid., 17.

[4] Ibid., 24.

[5] Nikos Kazantzakis, *The Last Temptation of Christ* (New York: Simon & Schuster, 1960).

[6] Mark 15:34 and parallels.

[7] Duff Cooper, *David* (out of print).

[8] Frank Slaughter, *David, Warrior and King* (New York: World Publishing Company, 1962).

[9] Laurene Chinn, *The Unanointed* (New York: Crown Publishers, Inc., 1958).

Chapter 24

God in the Plot

As implied in chapter 22, Bible stories are not the only stories that have God as a member of the cast. This, of course, applies to the written word as much as to word of mouth.

Charles Williams was another member of the Inklings. Out of his varied books, *War in Heaven*[1] is an example of a fiction in which God is one of the characters. It belongs to a class of novels described as "supernatural thrillers." It has all the ingredients of a murder mystery, but with a depth that such a mystery usually lacks. Williams explores the half-known world of the occult, and the half-seen world of the Spirit of God.

The book opens with a corpse lying strangled under an office desk. The scene is recounted with a grim humor that often recurs in the book to relieve the tension of the coming horror. For horror there is. The murder is the first step in a battle not only between human beings, but between the dark and the light spirit world that they serve.

Gregory Persimons, the retired publisher, has killed the man as an offering to Satan. He exults in the "power to enter those lives that he touches and twist them out of their security into a sliding destruction."[2] His immediate ambition is to offer an even better sacrifice, a living one, in the person of a small boy. To reach the child's mind, and more importantly his spirit, he gains possession of an antique chalice that proves to be the Holy Grail — the cup used by Jesus at the Last Supper. He hopes, rightly, that it has retained an aura of power, and he guesses that it can be used by either side.

Against him is the Archdeacon of Castra Parvulorum (a sleepy village known in the railway timetable as Fardles). He is a benign cleric who can often be heard muttering his favorite psalm: "O give thanks to the God of all gods; for his mercy endureth for ever."[3] The Grail happens to be the property of his parish church. He also (though to him it is no more than an inanimate thing) sees the possibility of its use by spiritual forces. (" 'Neither is this Thou,' he breathed; and answered, 'Yet this also is Thou.' ")[4]

Each has supporters and colleagues in various stages of faith in good or evil, and between them the uncommitted folk like the police inspector, whose "view of the devil was roughly that the devil was something in which children believe, but generally known not to exist."[5] The strange occurrences, when Gregory and his friends try to destroy the Grail by the force of thought, the great climax when the Archdeacon, bound and helpless, is subjected to a black magic that he cannot resist and that backfires on the perpetrators, make it clear that (for the purpose of the novel, at least) Satan is very real. Satan, however, is not quite so powerful as God; perhaps he is even the dark shadow of God. And when in the final chapter the Archdeacon dies peacefully at the altar, we cannot tell whether all the congregation has been hallucinating, or whether there really was a visit from Prester John, the timeless keeper of the Grail.

We can treat this fascinating book as a murder mystery (which it is); or as a piece of fantasy fiction (which it is). Either way, we cannot help thinking about God. The characters all have their own views of God, which are described with unusual skill. We follow both Gregory and the Archdeacon into states of mind in which they are aware of new worlds and invading spirits. We can treat that as fiction, but we wonder: is such a spirit world possible? We have to choose: faith or skepticism; and if faith, then faith in what or Whom?

If you set out to write such a book, beware of two dangers. First, there is the obvious danger of playing with fire. Can you handle the occult without being burnt? If you approach it in the spirit of faith in Jesus Christ, his promise will no doubt hold good that even "the gates of Hades" cannot stand up to the onslaught of his Church.[6] But you must be aware throughout your writing that the battle between heaven and hell is as real within yourself as in your fictitious characters. If you set out to attack the powers of evil, there is more than a possibility that you yourself will be the object of an attack as vicious as that inflicted on the Archdeacon of Castra Parvulorum.

A more subtle danger lies in the difficulty of making the plot credible. You are dealing with what, to many people, is not only fiction, but impossible fiction. The police inspector's view is far from unique to him. It requires a great integrity of writing to balance on the tightrope stretching between the horrific and the ridiculous. Williams achieves it partly by lightness of touch and more than a little humor. However doubtful we are of the existence of the plot's spiritual forces, we can enjoy reading of them and make them, for a little while at least, personal.

Of course, fiction can tell God's story in a direct way without such an exploration into the unseen world. It could be as simple as Agnes Sligh Turnbull's *The Bishop's Mantle.*[7] A young minister makes his mistakes and has his successes in daily life of a city parish. Occasionally he catches a flash of glory as he sees God acting through him. His story is told with gentleness and humor. It is easy reading, demanding little deep thought; but the reality of God shines through its plot. There is a danger of making God appear unreal. Perhaps this danger is inherent in any mention of God in a century of skepticism.

The narrative needs to ring true to the reader's experience, or capture the imagination. At the same time God's activity must not be superimposed, but must be an integral part of the plot. To write such a tale requires eyes that are open to God in the writer's daily life.

[1] Charles Williams, *War in Heaven* (Grand Rapids, Michigan; Wm. B. Eerdmans Publishing Co., 1949).

[2] Ibid. 71.

[3] Ibid. 43.

[4] Ibid. 137.

[5] Ibid. 221.

[6] Matthew 16:18.

[7] Agnes Sligh Turnbull, *The Bishop's Mantle* (New York: The Macmillan Company, 1947).

Chapter 25

Allegory

C.H. Dodd declared in *The Parables of the Kingdom* that Jesus never used allegory and that allegorical interpretations of the parables were added later by his disciples.

But first, what is the difference? A parable, he says, is "the natural expression of a mind that sees truth in concrete pictures rather than conceives it in abstractions."[1] One difference between Greek thought and Hebrew thought is that the Greeks made subtle abstract definitions, while Hebrew thinkers made the same statement by means of a parable. A parable has the added force of leaving the hearer compelled to make a decision. For example, Jesus clearly intends a decision when, after recounting the tale of the Good Samaritan, he adds, "Go and do likewise."[2]

An allegory, on the other hand, is a form of code, an expanded metaphor. But it is more than metaphor. Each detail has its own meaning, and it can be understood only if you have the key. A simple form of allegory is the political cartoon where, for example, a maple leaf or a Mounted Policeman stands for Canada, an eagle or the figure of Uncle Sam for the United States. Dodd quotes with scorn the allegorical interpretation that St. Augustine placed on this parable of the Good Samaritan:

> A certain man went down from Jerusalem to Jericho: Adam himself is meant; Jerusalem is the heavenly city of peace, from whose blessedness Adam fell; Jericho means the moon, and signifies our mortality, because it is born, waxes, wanes, and dies. Thieves are the devil and his angels. Who stripped him, namely, of his immortality; and beat him, by persuading him to sin; and left him half-dead, because in so far as man can understand and know God, he lives, but in so far as he is wasted and oppressed by sin, he is dead; he is therefore half-dead. The priest and Levite who saw him and passed by, signify the priesthood and ministry of the Old Testament, which could profit nothing for salvation. Samaritan means Guardian, and therefore the Lord Himself is signified by this name. The binding of the wounds is the restraint of sin. Oil is the comfort of good hope; wine the exhortation to work with fervent spirit. The beast is the flesh in which He deigned to come to us. The being set upon the beast is belief in the incarnation of Christ. The inn is the Church, where travelers are refreshed on their return from pilgrimage to their heavenly country. The morrow is after the resurrection of the Lord. The two pence are either the two precepts of love, or the promise of this life and of that which is to come. The innkeeper is the Apostle (Paul). The supererogatory payment is either his counsel of celibacy, or the fact that he worked with his own hands lest he

should be a burden to any of the weaker brethren when
the Gospel was new, though it was lawful for him "to
live by the Gospel." (Quaestiones Evangeliorum, II. 19
— slightly abridged.)[3]

No, Jesus probably did not have all this in mind. Some of
these interpretations might well be useful as sermon
illustrations; others strike us as exceedingly fanciful. But the
main objection to this whole pattern of interpretation is that
Jesus was not thinking here in allegorical terms at all.

This does not mean he never used allegory. Indeed, some of
his stories demand it. To a Jewish mind a vine or a fig-tree must
have carried a political significance like that of the maple leaf or
the stars and stripes today. A wedding-feast did not of necessity
refer to the Heavenly Banquet, yet the image did not originate
with Jesus. Indeed, Jesus would have had to avoid such
metaphors unless he intended the accepted allegorical code to
be applied to them.

Undoubtedly allegory is an honored and effective way of
telling God's story. It dresses old truths in new clothes, and
reaches depths of understanding that the simple statement of
those same truths would leave untouched.

Look, for example, at C.S. Lewis' children's novel, *The Lion,
the Witch and the Wardrobe.*[4] The author makes no pretense of
telling "truth" in the sense of historical fact. This is fairy-tale
pure and simple. Before the book is laid down, however, we
aware that the book is a life of Christ.

Four children have wandered into the magic
world of Narnia, which is under the spell of the

White Witch, and where it is "always winter and never Christmas." One of the four, Edmund, meets the witch, and is tempted by her offer of his favorite candy (magic, of course), which destroys his will power. He then betrays his brother and sisters to her.

The other three enlist with Aslan, the Great Lion, Son of the Emperor Oversea, to overthrow the usurper. Unfortunately, the Witch has the upper hand, for she claims the law of magic which gives her the right a slay a traitor. Aslan, recognizing the validity of this, arranges a private parley with her, and bargains away his life for Edmund's. To the horror of the two watching girls, he allows himself to be captured, mocked, tortured, and killed.

All night the Lion's bound body rests on the Stone Table, where he had been murdered. At dawn an army of mice nibbles away the cords and frees Aslan from death. Aslan springs up to a victory dance with the jubilant children and then, with a roar, advances to the battle. For, as he explains, there is a deeper magic: if an innocent party surrenders and becomes a willing substitute, death itself works backward.

Here is allegory. The code is clear: Aslan = Christ; the White Witch = the devil; the Stone Table = the Cross = death (it splits in two at Aslan's resurrection); winter = the curse, which is reversed with Aslan's victory, and so on, down to such details as Aslan's entrusting the conduct of the battle to his chosen people under Peter, the eldest of the children.

Edmund, of course, repents and is reinstated among the "saints," but without any melodrama or unreality. Lewis's skill in interpreting the Gospel in allegory is matched by his skill in maintaining our interest and acceptance. Even his "deception of the devil"[5] becomes both credible and just under Lewis's hand; for what child will not agree that the Witch met her just deserts in Aslan's use of the "deeper magic"?

Lewis did the same for adults with his trilogy of space fiction, especially *Voyage to Venus.*[5]

> Ransom (no doubt the name was deliberately chosen), in a previous volume was catapulted against his will to the dying civilization of Mars. He is then sent by forces bigger than himself to Venus, where life is being created. On Venus the scientist who kidnaped him is about to destroy the innocence of the newly formed woman. Ransom finds himself fighting verbally for her freedom, and fighting physically to destroy the evil power which has taken control of the scientist.

This series is not as successful as the children's series, partly because children are the audience *par excellence* for a story (and Lewis is at his best with them) and partly because space travel is now a reality. Lewis's very unsophisticated descriptions are suspect at once. Yet the Fall and Redemption of humanity are so clearly told that this book is also worth reading. It is a pleasurable story and a lesson in the use of allegory.

The examples in this chapter are both a warning and an encouragement for anyone who decides to write allegory. On one hand, the narrative must be compelling in itself; on the other, the code must be clear enough to understand without explanation. Lewis's novels make enjoyable reading, whether or not you see a deeper meaning through them. Jesus' parable of the Good Samaritan is known and loved throughout the world, whereas Augustine's detailed interpretation of it is irrelevant to a modern reader. Allegory must be transparent; it must not be an added extra. And every story must hold the reader's interest, regardless of any further purpose that the writer may have in telling it.

---

[1] C.H. Dodd, *The Parables of the Kingdom*, 15. See chapter 19, fn. 1.

[2] Luke 10:37.

[3] *The Parables of the Kingdom*, 11-12.

[4] C.S. Lewis, *The Lion, the Witch and the Wardrobe* (Oxford: The Bodley Head, 1950).

[5] See Gustav Aulen *Christus Victor*, authorized translation by A. G. Hebert, M. A., D.D. (London: S. P. C. K., 1953) 26.

[6] C.S. Lewis, *Perelandra* (New York: Macmillan, 1965. republished as *Voyage to Venus)*.

Chapter 26

Parable

A fourth member of the Inklings was J.R.R. Tolkien. The "hobbits" that he invented have passed into English lore.

> Hobbits are an unobtrusive but very ancient people, more numerous formerly than they are today; for they love peace and quiet and good-tilled earth: a well-ordered and well-farmed countryside was their favorite haunt.
>
> They are a little people, smaller than Dwarves.
>
> They dressed in bright colors, being noticeably fond of yellow and green; but they seldom wore shoes, since their feet had tough leathery soles and were clad in a thick curling hair, much like the hair of their heads, which was commonly brown.[1]

Tolkien said of himself:

> I cordially dislike allegory in all its manifestations, and
> always have done so since I grew old enough to detect
> its presence. I much prefer history, true or feigned, with
> its varied applicability to the thought and experience of
> readers. I think that many confuse 'applicability' with
> 'allegory'; but the one resides in the freedom of the
> reader, and the other in the purposed domination of
> the author.[2]

Recall the comments of Marcus Barth and of Robert
McAfee Brown, quoted in the first chapter: Barth's words: "it
leaves free both that which is narrated and the audience" and
McAfee Brown's: "it must 'stretch' me, pull me . . . open up
some new door . . . . " Tolkien also brings to minds Dodd's
dictum that the writer of parables "sees truth in concrete
pictures."

Tolkien's *The Hobbit*[3] and its longer sequel *The Lord of the
Rings* form a long parable, for they leave us with a choice that
must be made, just as truly as in Jesus' story of the Good
Samaritan.

> The tale is of a ring — of The Ring —
> In the Land of Mordor where the Shadows lie.
> One ring to rule them all, One Ring to find them,
> One Ring to bring them all and in the darkness bind
> them,In the Land of Mordor where the Shadows lie.[4]

This One Ring has strange powers. It makes its
wearer invisible; it also makes him visible to the Dark

Lord of Mordor and his agents. It confers long life; it also saps the will and grows greed. Frodo the Hobbit inherited it from his Uncle Bilbo and has been told by Gandalf the Grey Wizard to return it to its place of origin, the only place where it can be destroyed.

Gandalf's orders have a way of being obeyed. So Frodo and three companions set out on what proves to be a long, hazardous pilgrimage guided by a chance acquaintance, Strider the Ranger. From the start they are dogged by the Black Riders, who are determined to sniff out the Ring and regain it for their evil master.

Through six books the journey goes on, until Frodo and his faithful servant Sam have crossed the frontiers of Mordor itself and found the Cracks of Doom where the Ring was forged. The last book has Gollum, the depraved creature whose longing to lay his paws on the Ring has almost, but not quite, been cured, finally seize it and fall with it to his destruction. Gollum seizes it just as Frodo is overcome by its selfishness and decides to keep the ring for himself.

The sequel — the hobbits' return to their homeland, and the passing of the Ring-bearers into a world of eternity —adds little to the plot, but serves to round out the story and tidy up the loose ends. Tolkien succeeds in his long fictional story. The glimpse he gives of other stories — ancient chronologies and genealogies, vocabularies and scripts of the old days before human beings ruled, and hints of cosmic powers beyond those in the book — leave us with a tantalizing feeling that perhaps it is true after all. We are drawn into the war, unsuspiciously and inevitably. We travel with Frodo and share his hopes and his failures; and we, too, are pitted against the Darker Power, but what is that Darker Power? By what war can it be conquered, if indeed it can be finally conquered? The questions remain, haunting, unanswered. For suddenly we remember that the story is fiction and but that the Dark Powers surrounding us are fact.

The book leaves us with the reality of choice. Iaian Smith of *The Toronto Star* wrote:

> The heaviest task of the tale falls to Frodo, the humble but indomitable Hobbit here. In his resistance to the Fellowship of the Ring, and the evil Lord of Mordor, this generation of students identifies an echoing quality of its own dedication to freedom.[5]

Gandalf is a Christ-figure. (Not that his crotchety sense of humor tallies exactly with the character of Jesus of Nazareth.) Gandalf comes to dwell with hobbits for their salvation. He is always accessible to their cries for help. He wrestles with principalities and powers on their behalf and he lays down his life for his friends.

In spite of all this Tolkien does avoid falling into the allegory that he abhors, until Gandalf's resurrection. Here, for the first time, the tale rings false. Gandalf falls into the depths of the earth as he rescues his hobbit-friends from some elemental ogre of the deeps. We do not expect to see him again; but the story needs him. When he reappears, he explains how he has been dragged down into a near-annihilation, equal to Hades or Sheol. After a long sojourn there he has been given higher power than ever before, and is well on the way to claiming a "name that is above every name."[6] The code can be read: death leads to resurrection, and Gandalf = Christ. The parable has become an allegory.

If only Gandalf could have survived without the necessity of death (or apparent death?); or if only he could have died and remained dead. Tolkien has let melodrama in too. It is not possible that a wizard so good and so powerful should perish. He has to "escape in the final reel."

These criticisms are pin-pricks against the massive achievement of this work, but they serve to show how easily parable slips into allegory.

What is this but the skillful use of parable? And what is it but the story of God?

---

[1] J.R.R. Tolkien, *The Lord of the Rings* (in three volumes) (Toronto: George Allen & Unwin Ltd., 1954/55. one volume paperback, London: Unwin Paperbacks, 1978). 13-14).

[2] Ibid., 9.

[3] J.R.R. Tolkien. *The Hobbit, or There and Back Again* (London: Unwin Books, 1937).

[4] J.R.R. Tolkien, *The Lord of the Rings*, 5 (unnumbered).

[5] J.R.R. Tolkien. *The Fellowship of the Ring: Being the First Part of the Lord of the Rings* (London: George allen and Unwin, Ltd., 1954/55 reprinted Toronto: Methuen, 1971) inside front cover.

[6] Philippians 2:9.

Chapter 27

Living History

A further method of telling God's story is to write history as it happened. The broad sweep of history, ancient or modern is the sphere of God's action, as Herbert Butterfield made clear in *Christianity and History*.

> History must be a matter of considerable concern to Christians, . . . if now, as in Old Testament times, it is true that the real significances and values are not to be found by focusing our attention upon man in nature, but are to be sought rather by the contemplation of man – and the ways of God with man – in history."[1]

History as a science is the work of the specialist. But accounts of recent events, or stories of contemporary persons, are also history. There are all sorts of examples: biographies of the famous and the not so famous, records of special events found in missionary journals, church newspapers, and personal correspondence. Untold numbers of writers cut their teeth on local histories.

Like biblical narrative, this is also a tightrope. The essential
ingredient is research. To produce an accurate biography, for
example, it is not enough to admire, nor even to know, the
subject. Hours of pouring over letters, minutes, and diaries are
necessary to ensure that the facts are accurate. More hours are
required to sort the facts thus gleaned and to put them not only
into chronological order, but into a logical form. When all of
that is finished, you have a boring list of facts and statistics
unless imagination has been used. But imagination can be used
only within very strict limits, for you dealing not with a novel,
where historical inaccuracies may be pardoned, but with a life
story or an actual situation.

Godfrey Gower, the retired Archbishop of British
Columbia, undertook to write the history of Christ Church,
Surrey Centre. He stipulated that members of the parish must
do the research and present him with facts and figures. He
promised to add his own memories and to mold everything
together into a literary form. In his "Acknowledgments" at the
beginning of the volume he writes: "As I browsed through it all
the dusty past became a vivid present and the dead lived again,
exciting my admiration for the pioneers and the faith that
guided them."[3] And so the dates and statistics took shape as a
living story.

Such a local history may be of only local interest, but, as the
preface of the same book reminds us, "The history of our
nation is a collage of the little histories of our communities."[4]
The story of God may well be a collage of the biographies of
God's people.

God's people are windows through which you can see God.
To meet a woman or man of God can be an entry into the
presence of God. In a biography you can explore the working of

God's grace in someone else's life; you can watch God change the ugly into the beautiful. You can see God accomplish the impossible and thereby be encouraged to let God direct your own life.

There is one biography that shows the development, not so much of its subject's faith, as of the faith of those around the subject. It is the life of a two-year-old.[5] Actress Dale Evans, writing under her married name of Rogers, recounts the traumatic birth, life and death of a child with Down's syndrome. Her description of how the child, shortly before her death, "raised herself with great effort so that she could point at the picture of Jesus"[6] is touching enough; and the words of Father Smith: "You and your husband will soon begin to receive what our Lord wants you to learn from this child"[7] set the tone for the rest of the book: but something more was needed to raise the book from a tear-jerker into a masterpiece. That "something more" is the form in which the author tells it.

> Robin reports to God on her arrival back in heaven. "Oh, Father, it's good to be home again.[8] . . . They started doing all sorts of odd things to me to make me move around. They told each other that something was wrong," while all the time "this, too, was part of the Plan."[9] She goes on to describe the growing faith of her parents, until the day when, suffering from "mumps encephalitis," and running a temperature of 108, she suddenly finds relief: "You came, and I felt myself being lifted up."[10]
>
> "They're a lot stronger, since they got Our message," she finishes. "There's a new glory inside them and on everything all around them, and they've made

up their minds to give it to everybody they meet. The
sun's a lot brighter in Encino, since we stopped off
there for a while. And now, Father, please . . . could
I just go out and try my wings?[11]

Here is imagination that does not distort the facts. Is *Angel
Unaware* really the biography of Robin, or is it of Dale Evans
and Roy Rogers?

Another book that captured the attention of Christians
throughout the world is Betty Elliott's story of the mid-century
martyrs of Ecuador, *Through Gates of Splendor*.[12] The facts she
already knew, for she was a participant in the events. The power
of the story lies not simply in the setting — remote and exotic —
but in the "resurrection" quality of what could have been an
unrelieved tragedy.

> Five young Americans are determined to take the
> Gospel to the Auca Indians of Ecuador, a little-
> known tribe of killers. They start by gift-drops from a
> light aircraft. Then, after learning a little of the lan-
> guage and judging that their gifts are eroding the
> barrier of enmity and suspicion, they set up a bridge-
> head in the jungle. They build themselves a
> tree-house and call into the undergrowth to the ears
> they are certain are listening. Their wives, waiting for
> the daily radio transmissions, thrill to hear of the ar-
> rival of a man and two women, who walk into the
> camp and give every appearance of friendliness.
> Then, after the trio have left, all contact with the five
> men is lost.
> The civil authorities are alerted, and an expedi-
> tion is mounted to investigate. They reach the

tree-house to discover the fabric of the plane torn to shreds, and the five men stabbed to death.

The "resurrection quality" that I spoke of can be easily seen in the sequel, *The Savage My Kinsman*.[13] This book describes in words and pictures the bereaved wives' determination to keep faith with their husbands, to continue their efforts to reach the Aucas with the Word of Christ. One woman is given a welcome by the same people who murdered her husband. The book tells of the beginning of the conversion of the tribe to Christ. But this same spirit of hope and trust — this "resurrection" quality — runs through the account of the tragedy. And because there was someone there who put pen to paper to tell of it, the whole world learned of the martyrdom.

[1] H. Butterfield, *Christianity and History* (London: G. Bell and Sons Ltd., 1950) 2-3.

[2] *Echoes Through a Century*, the Centennial History of Christ Church, Surrey Centre, 1882-1982 (Cloverdale, B.C.: printed by D.W. Friesen, 6).

[3] Ibid. 5.

[4] Dale Evans Rogers, *Angel Unaware* (Fleming H. Revell Company, 1963. paperback, Jove Publications, 1977).

[5] Ibid., 11

[6] Ibid., 9

[7] Ibid., 21

[8] Ibid., 23

[9] Ibid. 63.

[10] Ibid. 64.

[11] Elisabeth Elliot, *Through Gates of Splendor* (Tyndale Press, 1981).

[12] Elisabeth Elliot, *The Savage My Kinsman* (Ann Arbor, Michigan: Servant Books, 1961).

Postscript

Jesus said to the healed demoniac: "Return home and tell how much God has done for you" (Lk 8:39).

John guessed that if all Jesus' actions were recorded, "the whole world would not have room for the books that would be written" (Jn 21:25).

So what's keeping you?

THE STORYTELLER'S LIBRARY

Storytelling Resources

Balloons! Candy! Toys! and Other Parables for Storytellers, by Daryl Olsziewski, **$8.95**

Storytelling Step by Step, by Marsh Cassady, **$9.95**

Telling Stories Like Jesus Did: Creative Parables for Teachers, by Christelle Estrada, **$8.95**

Other Story Collections

No Kidding God, Where Are You?, by Lou Ruoff, **$7.95**

For Give: Stories of Reconciliation, by Lou Ruoff, **$7.95**

The Magic Stone — and Other Stories for the Faith Journey, by James Henderschedt, **$7.95**

The Topsy Turvy Kingdom, by James Henderschedt, **$7.95**

Parables for Little People, by Larry Castagnola, **$7.95**

More Parables for Little People, by Larry Castagnola, **$7.95**

Angels To Wish By: A Book of Story Prayers, by Joseph J. Juknialis, **$7.95**

Winter Dreams: and Other Such Friendly Dragons, by Joseph J. Juknialis, **$7.95**

When God Began In the Middle, by Joseph J. Juknialis, **$7.95**

A Stillness Without Shadows, by Joseph J. Juknialis, **$7.95**

The Stick Stories, by Margie Brown, **$7.95**

A People Set Apart, by Jean Gietzen, **$6.95**

Breakthrough: Stories of Conversion, by Andre Papineau, **$7.95**

Jesus on the Mend: Healing Stories, by Andre Papineau, **$7.95**

Biblical Blues: Growing Through Setups and Letdowns, by Andre Papineau, **$7.95**

Ask for these titles at your local library or bookseller, or write to:

Resource Publications, Inc.
160 E. Virginia Street, Suite #290
San Jose, CA 95112-5848